Palmer/Pletsch

Sewing
ULTRASUEDE®

BRAND FABRICS

Ultrasuede®
Facile®
Caress™
Ultraleather™

by Marta Alto, Pati Palmer and Barbara Weiland

Book design, and production coordination, by Linda Wisner

Fashion illustrations by Diane Russell Kramer
Technical illustrations by Kate Pryka
Fashion photography by Carole Meyer assisted by Kim Meyer
Accessories by Cleo Cummings
Cover photo by Charles True
Book production by Strobeck Design

As always we owe our special thanks to associates and friends who contributed their special talents to this book. To Associates Marta Alto, Barbara Weiland, Lynn Raasch, Kathleen Spike, Terri Burns and Pati Palmer, thanks for the beautiful garments they sewed and loaned for the color photography. To student intern, Katherine Foster, and to Mike Spike, Ron Ellwanger, Melissa Palmer Watson and Stacy Alto, thanks for appearing as models. Thanks to custom dressmaker, Marla Kazel, for her sewing expertise and to dressmaker/designer, Pat Hagen, for her contributions in designing and sewing the trapunto and applique designs in the Ultraleather, Facile and Caress evening ensemble. We also owe our gratitude to Linda Wisner for her artistic eye and her patient management of the production and printing of the final manuscript. And to Lynette Ranney Black for keeping everything else under control for all of us.

And last, but not least, a special thanks to Barry Leonard, Vice President and General Manager, and Blair Roberts, Retail Sales Manager, of the Ultrasuede division of Springs Industries for their enthusiastic support and encouragement in the production of this book and the one-hour companion video.

Whenever brand names are mentioned, it is only to indicate to the consumer products which we have personally tested and with which we have been pleased. It is also meant to save our students time. There may be other products that are comparable to aid you in your sewing.

ISBN 0-935278-23-0

Table of Contents

Meet the Authors...

Palmer/Pletsch Associates has combined the talents of three fashion sewing experts to create the most up-to-date and practical book on sewing with the Ultrasuede family of fabrics—the original suitweight Ultrasuede, lightweight Facile, feather light Caress R and Ultraleather. **Pati Palmer** co-authored her first book on Ultrasuede when it made its debut in the early 1970s. **Marta Alto** has taught the Palmer/Pletsch Ultrasuede seminars nationwide and in Canada and stars in four Palmer/Pletsch videos on serging as well as in the companion video to this book. **Barbara Weiland** is a nationally known sewing editor, author and educator.

Barbara Weiland, Marta Alto and Pati Palmer

Pati Palmer is the owner and CEO of Palmer/Pletsch Associates, a company renowned for selling over 2 million books on home sewing subjects in the US, Canada, Australia and New Zealand. With her previous partner, Susan Pletsch, Pati created the a highly recognized line of personalized sewing patterns, first for Vogue and now for the McCall Pattern Company. In the past ten years, over 100 of her designs have appeared on the pages of the McCall's pattern catalog, many of them making it to the top ten best-seller list. Pati is the only publisher in the country who specializes in sewing books and videos. Her latest publishing venture is the creation of four-color serger idea books.

Marta Alto writes from her vast experience, having sewn hundreds of Ultrasuede garments. Her expertise makes her an invaluable addition to the Palmer/Pletsch design team. During her 23-year career, she has taught over 3000 sewing classes, so she knows how the home sewer thinks! Marta brings her artistic ability to every project she creates. She feels her innovative yet practical approach to sewing is a direct result of her early work as a historic costume technician for stage productions. Marta shares techniques that give speedy yet professional results.

Barbara Weiland is a former editor of SEW NEWS and the co-author of another best-selling Palmer/Pletsch book, **"Clothes Sense: Straight Talk About Wardrobe Planning."** Her articles appear regularly in national home sewing publications. In addition to teaching the Palmer/Pletsch method of sewing at four-day workshops held in Portland, Oregon, Barbara is the Publications Director for Palmer/Pletsch. Her special combination of teaching, writing and sewing expertise, make her an invaluable asset in the production of Palmer/Pletsch books, videos and the special guidesheets she develops for their line of patterns for McCall's. She is a multi-faceted sewing educator and communicator.

Foreword from Pati Palmer, President, Palmer/Pletsch Associates

Dear Sewing Enthusiast,

It's hard to believe that it's been almost twenty years since Ultrasuede® made its fashion debut in December, 1971. I had the privilege of sewing with Ultrasuede **before** it's introduction—it was only 36" wide then and sold for $16 a yard! Three years later, after lots of fun experimenting with this revolutionary new fabric, Susan Pletsch and I wrote our first book about sewing this fabulous faux suede fabric, **SEWING SKINNER® ULTRASUEDE FABRIC**. My talented associates and I have been sewing with it, wearing it, washing it, writing about it, and teaching others how to sew on it ever since.

The art of simulating real leather and suede has come a long way since the initial introduction of Ultrasuede. Many have tried similar products, but Ultrasuede still reigns supreme in appearance, hand, ease of sewing and seasonless appeal and wearability. And now, thanks to the same basic technology, there is not just one Ultrasuede, but a trio of three different weights from which to choose—classic suitweight Ultrasuede, mid-weight Facile®, and feather-light Caress™—PLUS the latest addition to the family, Ultraleather™, with a simulated leather face and a knit fabric backing.

It's interesting to note that the same microfiber technology that brought us Ultrasuede is still being explored. Polyester microfibers so fine that a mere pound of them can circle the earth at the equator (24,901.55 miles!), are now being woven into a whole new group of "Ultrafiber" fabrics, according to Barry Leonard, Vice President and General Manager of the Ultrasuede division of Springs Industries. Watch for them in truly luxurious versions of denim and washed silk looks as well as twill and gabardines. This new generation of fabrics is sure to complement your Ultrasuede garments!

We've taken the time to write this NEW book because we've learned lots more we'd like to share to give you the CONFIDENCE TO CUT and the INSPIRATION to try some new and creative ideas with any one (or all) of these wonderfully modern and still innovative fabrics. Inside these pages you'll find many of the tried and true methods we shared in that first book, PLUS updated techniques, information on new products that make it even easier to sew with the entire family of Ultrasuede fabrics, and lots of new ideas for making the most of your sewing time. We've added the excitement of fashion color photography for even more inspiration. And to make it even easier for you, we're offering a new one-hour companion video by the same title. We know you'll enjoy seeing Ultrasuede techniques and garments come to life in the talented hands of our resident Ultrasuede expert and instructor, Marta Alto. Watch for special instructions for Ultrasuede in the guidesheets of some of our **"Palmer/Pletsch Designer Details Made Easy"** patterns, too. You'll find them in the **McCall's** pattern catalog!

Our philosophy of sewing is it should be **FUN, FAST** and **EASY**. Notice "painful" was not mentioned. You shouldn't have to pray over something for six months before you can wear it. But...we also believe in a **professional** look. There is no room in really fine sewing for the look of "loving hands at home." The methods we share in this book are tried and true for Ultrasuede. There are other suitable methods, but these are what we have found to be the fastest, easiest and the most fun. We'll hold your hand as you cut into this expensive fabric. Use our book as a reference book and security blanket!

If this is your first time sewing with Ultrasuede fabrics, we know you'll be pleased with the experience and the results. If you're an avid fan already, we hope you'll explore some of the new and creative ideas in our book. We'd love to hear from you and to see photos of your efforts!

Happy Sewing

Pati Palmer

Pati Palmer,
President, Palmer/Pletsch Associates

INTRODUCTION:
Ultrasuede, The Ultimate Prestige Fabric!

Ultrasuede is an amazing suede-like fabric that looks, feels, moves and even sounds like real suede. The only thing it doesn't do is smell like suede—a real plus by our standards! Made using patented technology, seven years in development, this nonwoven wonder fabric is made of microfibers in a blend of 60% polyester and 40% nonfibrous polyurethane.

Ultrasuede is the ultimate prestige fabric. In 1972, the American designer, Halston, introduced Ultrasuede to the world of high fashion with his shirtdress—the hot status symbol that every Halston fan HAD to have. Ultrasuede quickly became one of Halston's hallmarks. In a recent article honoring the now deceased designer, Women's Wear Daily credited him with popularizing Ultrasuede in both apparel and luggage.

"The Ultrasuede Halston dress 'was...a huge success,' said Andrew Goodman, chairman of the executive committee at Bergdorf Goodman. 'I remember....we sold hundreds of them. Everybody else had turned down Ultrasuede. Seventh Avenue believed in playing it safe, but Halston had sense enough to know what a huge success it was. He was an unusual character.'"

We salute Halston for his vision and thank him for the important role he played in popularizing Ultrasuede and convincing other exclusive American designers—like Bill Blass and Anne Klein—not to mention the consuming public, how wonderful it really is. Ultrasuede has truly become an American classic. You'll find it used in everything from men's and women's apparel to footwear, millinery, furniture, luggage—even wall coverings—all with great style and aplomb!

So What Makes Ultrasuede So Wonderful?

Ultrasuede has the expensive look of the finest quality animal suede without any of suede's inherent disadvantages. It's now readily and regularly available in a wide range of classic neutrals and fashion shades, as well as seasonal colors introduced and rotated through the line as fashion dictates.

Because of its unique nonwoven structure, Ultrasuede doesn't require any difficult or complicated sewing or finishing techniques. Like real suede, the raw edge of the fabric can be used as the finished edge. That means you have even more sewing options. You can choose to sew an Ultrasuede garment using the **conventional method** following your pattern guidesheet or you can choose **flat method** construction which is often faster and easier—with the added bonus of requiring less yardage.

Remember the other unique properties of Ultrasuede and take advantage of them.

- Ultrasuede doesn't water spot or stiffen; it always remains soft and supple.

  What could be more posh than a suede raincoat in a spring shower? You may want to spray it with a water repellent if you live in areas where heavy rains are prevalent. In Portland, Oregon, our misty rains just roll right off the napped surface.

- Ultrasuede is lightweight and wrinkle resistant. It won't shrink, bag or stretch, retaining shape wearing after wearing. Wrinkles just fall right out. Ultrasuede garments make perfectly packable travel wardrobes.

- Ultrasuede is **machine washable** and can be **tumble dried.**

  If you've ever wanted a cream colored blazer, here's your chance. You probably wouldn't dare in real suede because of the dry cleaning bills!

- Ultrasuede is colorfast and crock resistant.

  Ultrasuede belts won't leave color on your skirt waistband—and they won't stretch out of shape either. Belts are easy first projects in Ultrasuede—many are no-sew, cut-and-go projects!

- Ultrasuede is a seasonless fabric.

  It makes the perfect jacket for our often over-air conditioned restaurants and offices. Sew Ultrasuede garments that you can wear year 'round for maximum enjoyment. It's amazingly durable and often outlasts the life of a fashion trend so you can sew with the confidence that it won't be outdated before you've gotten a good return on your investment.

Men's sports coats are smashing in Ultrasuede and we love the versatility of an Ultrasuede coat. We think one belongs in every wardrobe because it's lightweight yet durable, doesn't wrinkle and can be worn comfortably over clothing layers. We often add a warm, button-in liner to our Ultrasuede coats for travel to colder climates. Then they make truly seasonless wardrobe additions. And Ultrasuede coats can look very dressy or very tailored depending on pattern choice and the construction method you choose.

In addition Ultrasuede:

• can be dry-cleaned by conventional methods.

• can be ironed on the wrong side using a press cloth and a steam iron on a synthetic setting.

• won't crock, nick, pill or fray. It's ALMOST indestructible!

Ultrasuede is a Good Investment

We firmly believe that buying and sewing Ultrasuede is a worthwhile investment of both your time and your money. If you're like us, sewing time has become one of life's luxuries so it's important to make the most of it. That's why we like to sew with fabrics like Ultrasuede. Every time you make a garment from a special fabric or one with special designer detailing, you can safely multiply your costs by seven and come up with the price you might find on a ready-made garment of **comparable** quality. For example, a tailored Ultrasuede jacket that cost you $175 to make could carry a designer price tag of over $1000! (NOTE: $175 is probably the **most** you would ever spend making an Ultrasuede jacket. If you take advantage of sales, an Ultrasuede jacket can cost much less.)

Think of Ultrasuede as a "gourmet" fabric. It may cost more per yard than most other fabrics in your wardrobe but it's important to remember that the price you pay is an initial expense only. It might cost you as much to make an Ultrasuede garment as it would a garment of real suede, but you will never have to pay the high cost of dry cleaning real suede—or deal with all the imperfections! Over the lifetime of your garment, the savings are substantial!

While Ultrasuede is not "new" anymore, it is still considered "amazing" by designers and fashion-sewers alike who adore its luxurious appeal as much as its easy-to-sew and easy-care advantages. And, we realize, Ultrasuede is always new to those home-sewers who have just taken the plunge and bought their very first piece. We know that heady feeling well! We can all remember taking the first piece out of the closet more than once, then admiring it, stroking it and putting it back for another day. We know it takes courage and encouragement to cut into it the first time! That's why we wrote this book!

How This Book is Organized

The emphasis in this book is on flat method construction for Ultrasuede because it is so different, but conventional methods are also included. While flat methods can sometimes be used for sewing Facile, we generally use conventional sewing. Caress and Ultraleather are both sewn conventionally. For additional information on sewing Facile, Caress and Ultraleather, refer to the special chapters on these fabrics at the end of the book.

Whether you're a member of longstanding or you've just joined or are thinking about joining the elite group of high-fashion home-sewers who love the challenge of sewing with any one of the Ultrasuede family of fabrics, this book contains the assistance, encouragement and inspiration you need to plan and sew beautiful, couture garments that you'll be proud to wear for years to come. So let's get on with what is bound to be a wonderful sewing adventure—even if you're already a pro at sewing this lightweight, wrinkle-resistant and truly seasonless fabric.

CHAPTER 1:
Selecting a Pattern for Ultrasuede

Now the fun begins! Besides a terrific, tailored jacket, you can sew any number of beautiful garments and accessories from Ultrasuede fabric. We've seen it used for everything from tablecloths (a great gift for the affluent bachelor on your list) to gorgeous handbags and ever-so-practical tote bags.

Pati was in a Portland furniture store and glancing to her side, discovered she was standing next to a chic sofa upholstered in the same color Ultrasuede she was wearing. While you might not go to that extreme, consider throw pillows or a lap robe pieced from Ultrasuede scraps. We've used it for director's chair covers and Marta patched her son's jeans with it! Why, we've even heard about Ultrasuede-upholstered jet interiors! One of our associates, Linda Wisner, used Ultrasuede Facile on the walls in her library/study—cozy and elegant combined with other Ultrasuede room accessories! See it pictured in **CREATIVE SERGING FOR THE HOME**, using a wonderful new product, Quik Trak, that makes it a "snap" to cover walls in fabric. Directions are included.

Let your imagination soar! And, tune in to ready-to-wear mail-order catalogs and fashion magazines for inspiration. That's where we get some of our best ideas for exciting Ultrasuede projects.

Basic Pattern Selection Guidelines

Simplify pattern selection by thinking of Ultrasuede as a medium-weight fabric much like crisp linen suiting. At times pattern catalogs feature special patterns for synthetic suedes or add extra tips to their guidesheets for sewing with them, but basically, any pattern can be adapted if it suits the features and weight of Ultrasuede.

1. For a first Ultrasuede project, start with something simple—a belt, an easy vest, a handbag or a simply styled jacket.

2. Look for **minimum easing**. Ultrasuede fabric, like real suede, will ease only 1" in 10". Even so, set-in sleeves ARE appropriate and we'll show you a slick trick to make them easier in Ultrasuede. Consider kimono, raglan, dropped shoulder and sleeveless styles as well. A few gathers at the wrist of a cuffed sleeve are OK, but you may want to

convert the fullness to pleats for a more tailored look. Designs with lots of gathering at waistlines and yokes add bulk to your figure. Save gathered styles for softer Facile and Caress.

3. Change front darts, which tend to bubble and "pooch'" over the tummy, to soft gathers or pleats in fitted skirts and pants. Consider skirt styles in gentle A-line shapes, with or without gores, if a straighter, fitted skirt is not your style. Avoid full and circular styles. They won't drape gracefully and they add lots of weight to the wearer—save them for Facile or Caress.

4. Tailored jackets and coats are naturals in Ultrasuede. Read the pattern description carefully. Slightly and loosely fitted styles are more attractive and appropriate for Ultrasuede. Nipped-in, overly curved side seaming from bustline to hipline is not appropriate. Avoid styles with overly curved seaming in the bustline area.

5. If you are larger than a "C" bra cup size, choose a pattern with bustline darts or add a dart for a better fit. Watch for designs with gently curved princess seaming extending up into to the shoulder seam or a front yoke rather than those that curve abruptly into the armhole. A LITTLE soft fullness from a yoke may work, too, for fuller figures.

6. Avoid "For Knits Only" patterns. They rely on the fabric stretching for comfort and fit. Ultrasuede has no more give than woven fabric.

7. The shirtdress is still a possibility in unbelted, straight-fitting styles but we agree that most dresses are more attractive, comfortable and appealing on all body types and in most pattern styles when sewn from Facile or Caress instead. Dresses and shirts drape better, flow more gracefully over body curves and are easier to wear in these softer fabrics.

8. Pattern styles with several narrow panels or designs with lots of little pieces usually take less yardage than those with larger pattern pieces, especially for flat construction. The pieces of a two-piece sleeve can often be squeezed into what would be wasted areas in a woven fabric pattern layout.

How Much Ultrasuede Yardage Should I Buy?

We hear this question a lot and we wish there was a magic formula—but there isn't one. Of course, you can always play it safe and buy the yardage specified on the pattern envelope, being careful to use the 45", "with nap" information. Then, if you decide to use flat rather than conventional construction, you'll have leftover yardage for a coordinating belt, one of Marta's easy little bags (page 38) or for trim on another garment. Small pieces are great in Ultrasuede patchwork and applique projects.

> **PRO TIP:** Because pattern companies now use computers to plan pattern layouts, we've discovered there is often less fabric waste in the layouts. If you follow the pattern yardage block, we don't recommend scrimping on yardage. It's better to do a test layout if you're really interested in saving on yardage. See below.

Preplanning saves money—from $5.00 to $50.00! If you spend a little extra time working out the details of your sewing project first, you can determine and purchase **exactly** the amount of Ultrasuede you'll need for **your pattern choice**, in **your size**, and for the **construction method** you wish to use.

How to Save on Yardage Needs

1. **Read this entire book first.** You'll find fabric-saving ideas throughout. And, some of our creative ideas that you may wish to incorporate when planning your project may affect yardage needs, too.

2. Select and purchase your pattern and **make all necessary fitting changes**. See pages 29 to 31.

3. Decide on the construction method you will use—conventional, flat or a combination. See pages 13 to 19.

4. Prepare the pattern pieces for the construction method you will use. Trim away all excess pattern tissue margins. Yes, this takes time but it makes it much easier to determine just how much yardage you'll need.

- **Conventional Method:** You can purchase the fabric according to the pattern yardage block for 45"-wide, "with nap" fabrics. However, Marta suggests a trial layout, even when using conventional sewing methods because you may be able to adjust the layout by tilting the pattern pieces. See below. In addition, Ultrasuede is actually 47" to 48" wide, a nice bonus in pattern layouts.

- **Flat Method:** Trim or fold back the seam and hem allowances that you won't need following the guidelines on page 15. Then **do a test layout.** Lay out the trimmed tissue pattern on a premarked cutting board to determine **exactly** how much yardage you'll need. By eliminating unnecessary seam and hem allowances, the pattern pieces will be much smaller and will fit into smaller spaces so you can buy less yardage. Be sure to read "Tips for Trial Layouts," below, first.

> **QUICK TIP:** Marta suggests buying a 3-yard piece of muslin or gingham to keep on hand for trial pattern layouts for **any** fabric that costs more than $10.00 per yard. Woven gingham has the advantage of built-in grainline markings. Of course, you can also raid your fabric stash for a 3-yard length to "borrow" or put into permanent service for trial layouts. (If you're like us, you probably have fabrics stashed that you know you'll never sew into finished garments. They're great candidates for this purpose!)

Tips for Trial Layouts

Your trial layout becomes your final layout. As you do your trial layout, keep these tips in mind to conserve yardage, save money and, in some cases, to add design interest to your Ultrasuede sewing project.

1. Ultrasuede is nonwoven but it does have directional differences. The lengthwise direction has the least stretch. Crosswise and bias give are similar but the most give is in the crosswise direction. That means pieces that need to be cut on the bias in a woven fabric can be cut on the crosswise direction of Ultrasuede fabric and that **saves yardage**!

2. Because of the crosswise give, garments should be cut with the crosswise grain going **around** the body for wearing comfort. If you want the nap of the **waistband** to match the garment, it must be cut on the **crosswise grain** of the fabric. The same is true of cuffs or hip bands. You will often to ignore the original grainline directions shown on the pattern tissue. It's **legal** with Ultrasuede!

3. Ultrasuede is a napped fabric so follow a **with nap** layout but you can **tilt** pattern pieces up to a 45° angle without any really noticeable color or shading differences. That helps **save yardage**, too. The slight nap variation created by tilting pattern pieces often adds to the appeal of the finished garment, making it look more like real suede with lights and darks at different angles.

4. Determine the desired finished length for the garment (and sleeves). Plan for cut-on hem allowances for conventionally sewn garments, but for flat construction, you can use the raw edge as the finished bottom edge or you can cut hem facings from scraps. Facings that won't show on the right side of the garment can be cut wherever you can fit them between other larger garment pieces without worrying about the direction of the nap.

5. Separating cut-on facings from the body of the garment may make it easier to conserve on yardage. You'll probably be able to slip the facing piece into a smaller space somewhere in the layout.

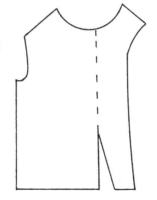

Facings and waistbands can also be pieced from scraps if necessary. If you must piece the waistband, add a creative touch so it looks like it was an intentional part of the design and not a mistake in cutting.

6. Patterns with lots of seams often save on yardage. Little pattern pieces can be squeezed into unbelievable spaces, especially when you can tilt them. And straight edges of pattern pieces can often be butted right against each other to save yardage and cutting time.

7. Don't be afraid to piece garment sections. Real suede garments are often pieced in order to make best use of the skins or to create visual differences in color and shading. The seams joining the pieces take on design importance and can be emphasized with topstitching.

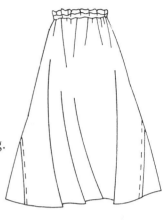

8. You can usually save even more yardage with a single layer layout. (UGH! We hate them, too, but this is one case where we might resort to them—to save money or to squeeze something out of existing yardage after we've changed our minds about what we want to make.) Be sure to plan the layout carefully so you cut **right and left halves**—or you won't save anything, including your sanity! Take your time!

When you've completed the test layout, measure to determine the exact yardage you'll need. Leave the pattern pieces pinned to the test fabric until you are ready to transfer them to the Ultrasuede. Or you can do a sketch or take an instant snapshot of the layout for reference later.

Construction Methods for Ultrasuede

Choose from two basic construction methods for your Ultrasuede garment—CONVENTIONAL or FLAT. In some garments you will use a combination of the two for sewing ease and wearing comfort. Let garment design and personal preference guide your choice of construction methods.

You'll find conventional seaming in most ready-to-wear Ultrasuede garments because factories are set up for this type of sewing. We think flat construction is faster and easier for many styles in Ultrasuede. And the garments look more like real suede.

Flat Method

Flat construction seems to be the easiest for first-time Ultrasuede sewers. Seams are less bulky and construction pressing is minimal, a nice plus!

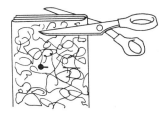

It also saves on yardage (and cost!) because you eliminate some seam and hem allowances. Garments made with flat seaming can look quite sporty with a row of edgestitching and a row of topstitching on all major seams. **Edgestitching only** is usually a dressier look in flat construction. There are also some creative treatments that can be done in flat construction.

Before doing any stitching on your garment, be sure to read **"STITCHING TIPS"** on page 32.

Garment Characteristics - Flat Method

1. No seam allowances on outer edges of collars, lapels, front edges and collarless necklines.

2. Lapped and stitched seams and darts.

3. Stitched and slashed or topstitched "window" bound buttonholes.

4. No hem allowances.

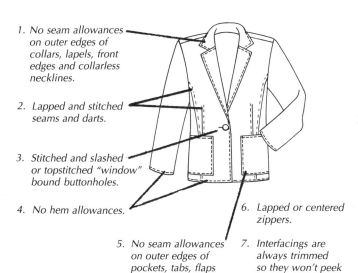

5. No seam allowances on outer edges of pockets, tabs, flaps and other applied details.

6. Lapped or centered zippers.

7. Interfacings are always trimmed so they won't peek out at raw edges.

PRO TIP: Don't let all the stitching scare you. The stitching usually blends right into the napped surface. Practice first on scraps.

Flat Seaming Tips

You'll use narrow strips of fusible web to steam-baste garment sections together for flat construction. This sheer fusing agent melts between two fabric layers to bond them together. Brands include Dritz Stitch Witchery® (also from HTC), Pellon Wonder Web™, Fuse and Use by J & R, and Jiffy Fuse by Staple Sewing Aids. Steam-basting takes the place of pinning and prevents seam slippage while stitching.

Buy web by the yard and cut your own strips—it's less expensive. Save time by folding a yard of fusible web into fourths and pin. Cut 1/4"-wide strips. Don't worry if strips are not exactly the same width. Keep handy in a small box or baggie.

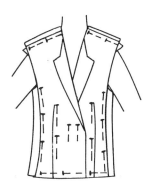

1. Trim away 5/8" seam allowance on the overlap half of each seam. Leave a full 5/8" seam allowance on the underlap half. Refer to "Pattern Preparation for Flat Construction," (page 16) for which edge should be the overlap and which the underlap half of each seam.

overlap   *underlap*

trim off 5/8"

seamline

2. Pin the body of the garment together to test fit. Lap cut edges to the 5/8" stitching line on each seam. Place pins parallel to raw edge. Try on and adjust the fit, repinning as needed.

3. Take off garment. On WRONG SIDE, mark the placement of each underlap seam edge and dart along the raw edges using a chalk or sharp lead pencil. Unpin after all lap positions are marked.

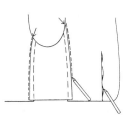

4. Working from WRONG SIDE, steam-baste one seam at a time. Place a narrow strip of fusible web on WRONG SIDE of **overlap** close to raw edge. Hold iron just above web; steam until it's just tacky enough to stick to the fabric.

5. Line up the raw edge of underlap at the line marked after fitting (steps 2 and 3, above). Using a press cloth, press lightly with a steam iron for 2 to 3 seconds to "baste" the layers together.

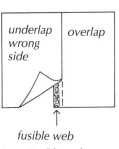

underlap wrong side | overlap

fusible web

Note: Fusible web should be right at raw edge.

FIT TIP: Steam-baste the body of a garment for one last fit check if desired. To make changes, gently pull steam-basted seams apart, scratch away the unmelted web, adjust the fit and fuse again using a new strip of web. Use rubbing alcohol to remove stubborn bits of web.

6. Edgestitch.

7. Topstitch 1/4" away if desired.

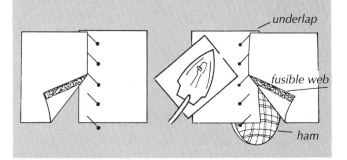

edgestitch | edgestitch and topstitch

PRO TIP: Pati often finds it easier to work from the **right side,** especially for shaped seams. Stick pins into garment vertically to mark seamline on the underlap side of seam. Steam-baste overlap in place 1" at a time. Use your fingers to smooth in the ease if needed. **Do this only with great care and caution and ALWAYS with a wool or napped press cloth!!!!!**

underlap

fusible web

ham

QUICK TIP: When edgestitching **and** topstitching, save time by stitching in a "U" at hem edges. Not so many knots to tie and hide!

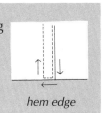

hem edge

Creative Ideas for Flat Construction

Substitute a decorative scalloping stitch for the topstitching in flat construction. It adds a delicate, feminine finish and you'll get lots of compliments! Use it on belts, around neckline and hem edges on a jacket, and as a decorative accent on patch pockets, cuffs and collars. Experiment with other decorative stitches, too. Serging raw edges using a decorative thread in the upper looper is another creative possibility.

For **lapped seams,** scallop stitch 1/16" inside the overlap edge so needle doesn't miss the fabric. (It's not pretty!) Trim around scallops. Use very sharp, double-pointed scissors. Be careful not to cut the stitches. Steam-baste overlap in place. Topstitch. Use inner points of scallops as stitching guideline.

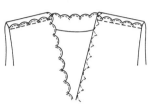

For **edges,** steam-baste facing and garment layers together, then scallop stitch and trim around the scallops.

Serger Flat Construction

edgestitch

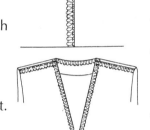

For **lapped seams,** decoratively serge overlap edges. Lap and steam-baste in place. Edgestitch through serging.

For outer **edges,** decoratively serge around garment after steam-basting facing to garment.

For lots of decorative serging inspiration, you'll want our **"Serger Idea Book."** See page 127 for more information.

Preparating Pattern for Flat Method Construction

In flat construction, which seam allowance becomes the overlap and which the underlap is really a matter of personal choice. Follow our guidelines as a general rule but don't be afraid to make changes when appropriate. As you read through the list compare it to our illustrations on page 16.

Flat Construction Guidelines

- **Front shoulder** overlaps back shoulder.

- **Front side seam** overlaps back, unless there's horizontal bustline dart. Then lap the back over front to hide dart ends for a neater finish.

- **Left back** overlaps right back at center back. We usually cut both backs the same, then trim away the seam allowance on the left back.

- **Front sleeve seam** overlaps back. Use armhole notches to tell front from back.

- **Upper sleeve** overlaps both seams on the under sleeve in a two-piece sleeve.

- **Sleeve bands** and **cuffs** overlap sleeves.

- **Dropped shoulder** overlaps flat sleeve cap.

- **Waistbands** overlap skirts and pants.

- **Concave curved edges** overlap convex curves as in princess seams.

- **Neckline bands** overlap the garment front and back neckline.

- **Collar bands** overlap the collar.

- **Collar** overlaps the neckline when a neckband is not included. However, we recommend conventional seaming to join collar to neckline.

- **Front** and **back yokes** overlap garment.

- **Straight edges** overlap eased, slightly gathered or pleated edges. Cut gathered edges with full 5/8" seam allowances.

The following are usually finished with cut edges in flat construction.

- Collars, lapels and front edges in coats, jackets and dresses.

- Outer edges of collars, patch pockets, flaps and tabs.

- Cuffs. One-piece cuffs may have a fold at the bottom edge. Two-piece cuffs have a raw edge at all four edges.

- Collarless necklines and sleeveless armholes.

- Jacket and coat hems are usually faced and edgestitched. A raw edge, with or without stitching is favored on skirts.

- Belts.

Prepare the Pattern for Flat Method Construction

1. Make all necessary fitting adjustments for your figure to the tissue paper pattern first.

2. Trim away or fold back the seam allowances on the pattern tissue in the amount indicated on the following edges.

3. Re-mark notches on the 5/8" seamline before trimming.

SKIRT WITH YOKE

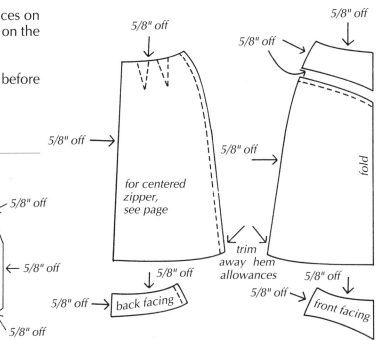

VEST

SHIRTDRESS OR SHIRT-STYLE JACKET

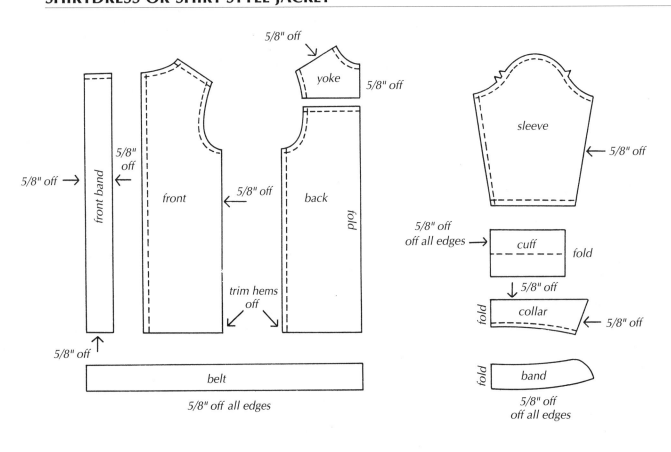

16

FITTED SKIRT

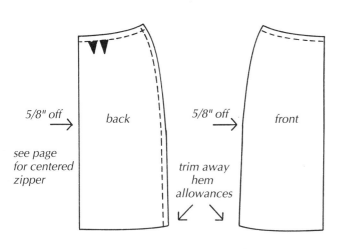

5/8" off → *back*

see page for centered zipper

5/8" off → *front*

trim away hem allowances

NOTE: For lapped zipper, leave both center back seam allowances on tissue and see page for application method.

PANTS WITH FLY FRONT

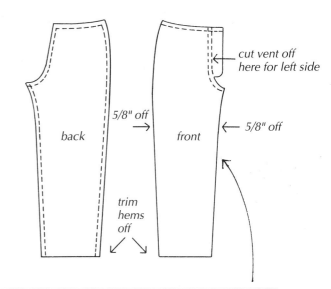

back

5/8" off →

front

← 5/8" off

cut vent off here for left side

trim hems off

NOTE: For ease in sewing, sew inseams conventionally if you prefer. Then leave this seam in tact.

MAN'S OR WOMAN'S BLAZER-STYLE

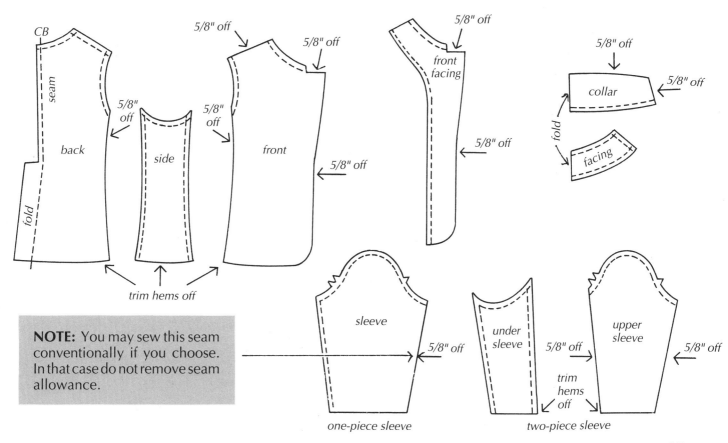

CB
seam
fold
back
5/8" off →
side
5/8" off
front
← 5/8" off
← 5/8" off

5/8" off
front facing
5/8" off

5/8" off
collar
← 5/8" off
fold
facing

trim hems off

sleeve
← 5/8" off
one-piece sleeve

under sleeve
5/8" off →
trim hems off
upper sleeve
← 5/8" off
two-piece sleeve

NOTE: You may sew this seam conventionally if you choose. In that case do not remove seam allowance.

Conventional Method

Create a garment with a classic or dressy appearance using conventional seaming and hemming throughout.

Conventional seaming takes more time than flat construction because it requires more careful pressing and trimming but the results can be quite elegant.

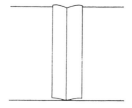

Garment Characteristics - Conventional Method

1. Standard 5/8"-wide seam allowances are stitched RIGHT SIDES TOGETHER and pressed open. Topstitched and mock welt seams are options. See page 19.

2. Collar and facing edges have enclosed seams.

3. Hems are turned and pressed, then fused or hand stitched.

4. Lapped, centered or fly front zippers.

5. Machine or bound buttonholes.

Follow the sequence of construction in the pattern guidesheet. The conventional method treats Ultrasuede like any other fabric.

Conventional Seaming Tips

1. Hold seams together for conventional sewing with FINE PINS or BASTING TAPE. This double-faced tape holds the layers together and prevents seam slippage. See **STITCHING TIPS** on page 32.

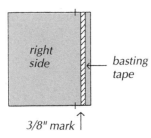

3/8" mark ↑

Place 1/8" wide basting tape 3/8" from the cut edge and remove the protective paper.

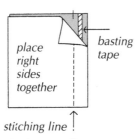

stitching line ↑

Stick seam allowances right sides together.

2. Stitch at 5/8" seamline using 10-12 stitches per inch.

3. Gently pull seam allowances apart and remove basting tape if you used it.

4. Press seams open over the flannel (napped fabric) side of a seam roll. Flatten seam with a tailor's clapper.

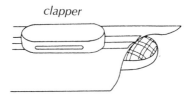

clapper

It is usually necessary to press and flatten a conventional seam **two to three times** to get a good press. Use a see-through press cloth on the wrong side and a heavier, **napped press cloth** when pressing from the **right side**. Keep top pressing to a minimum to avoid damaging the nap.

5. Press any enclosed seams open over a point presser or the June Tailor Board before turning.

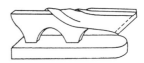

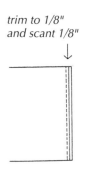

trim to 1/8"
and scant 1/8"
↓

6. Grade enclosed seams to reduce bulk AFTER pressing them open. It's easier. Because Ultrasuede doesn't ravel, you can safely trim seams to 1/8" and slightly narrower on the second layer.

PRO TIP: The very best advice we can give is to TAKE YOUR TIME—don't rush! Sew and press several seam test samples to get comfortable with the fabric.

Creative Ideas for Conventional Seams

For additional design interest:

Topstitch seam allowances, stitching 1/8" to 1/4" away from seamline. You may need to fuse seams in place to keep them from crawling while topstitching. **Test !**

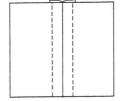

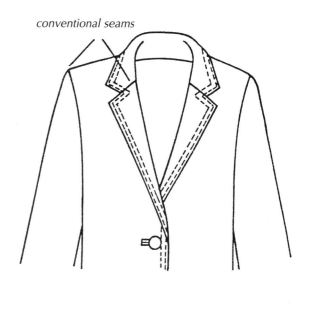

conventional seams

underlayer trimmed

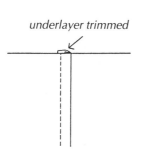

Press and topstitch seam allowances to one side for a **mock welt seam.** Trim the seam allowance next to the garment to 1/8" before topstitching to eliminate bulk.

Combination Method

There may be times when sewing is easier and the garment will be more comfortable to wear if you combine conventional and flat sewing methods. Or, you may prefer the appearance of conventional seaming on some seams and flat in others.

In most garments, we prefer to sew the following seams conventionally:

1. Set-in sleeves. It's easier to sew most sleeve seams with a conventional seam. It usually looks better and you get greater wearing comfort. However, the flatter sleeve caps in dropped shoulder designs and kimono and some raglan sleeve styles may be easier with flat method construction. See page 61.

2. Collar to neckline seams in jackets, coats and tailored shirtdresses. We prefer the clean appearance, especially in notched collar and lapel styling where the seam is really visible and gets lots of wear.

3. Crotch seam in pants. This is a sturdier and more comfortable seam when sewn conventionally. See page 58 for more pants sewing tips.

4. Most really curved seams are easier to sew with conventional seaming.

You may also prefer conventional sewing for the following seams:

1. Sleeve underarm seams. It takes more time and patience to sew a flat seam in a tube. Barbara always sews the underarm of a one-piece sleeve or the inside seam (closest to the underarm) in a two-piece sleeve this way. Marta prefers the flat method for BOTH sleeve seams in a two-piece sleeve. Guess who has more patience!

2. Pant inseam. It's faster and avoids sewing in a tube.

3. Marta usually sews vertical jacket darts with flat, lapped construction but prefers the appearance of a conventional dart for horizontal bustline darts. You may prefer the consistency of sewing all conventional darts in both conventional and flat construction garments. Experiment with samples and decide which look you like best.

CHAPTER 4:
Fabric Preparation, Cutting and Marking

Fabric Preparation

Shrinkage is negligible in Ultrasuede because of its unique construction and composition. If you wish to preshrink it anyway, follow the care instructions on page 105.

It may be advisable to preshrink other fabrics and notions used inside your Ultrasuede garments.

- **Fusible interfacings**—Preshrink woven, knit and weft-insertion fusible interfacing using the method described on page 27.

> **PRO TIP:** Do not preshrink fusibles of any type in your washer and dryer as the fusible resins will loosen and fall away.

- **Linings and underlinings**—Preshrink washable support fabrics by machine-washing and drying. It's so easy, why take a chance? **Some polyester linings do shrink.** Water temperature and dryer heat are both factors. When using a dry-cleanable lining fabric, steam press thoroughly before cutting to minimize the possibility of shrinkage.

DO NOT SHRINK FUSIBLE WEB!!!

Layout and Cutting

1. Be sure to review "Tips for Trial Layouts" on page 10, even if you didn't do a trial layout to determine yardage. In addition, because Ultrasuede has a nap, you have one more decision to make. Which way do you want the nap to run in the finished garment?

To make the decision easier, place the length of the fabric around your neck in front of a mirror. Notice how it looks richer and darker on the side where the nap runs up and lighter and softer where the nap runs down. Which do you prefer?

Barbara always cuts with the nap down for a softer look and Pati does the reverse. **Both** are **right.** After deciding on the nap direction, place a pin at one end of the yardage to designate the top.

2. Ultrasuede can be cut double layer for speed. Fold with the right sides out (wrong sides together) for speedier marking.

3. Use extra-fine, glass-headed pins pushed vertically through the pattern and fabric into the cutting board. Use only a few pins—four pins per piece is often enough. **Pinholes WILL disappear** when the fabric is steamed. If you prefer, use pattern weights to hold the pattern in place and cut out on a mat with a rotary cutter.

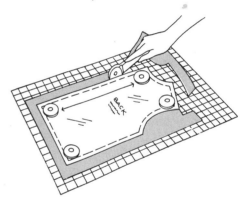

4. **Before taking the first cut,** check your layout one last time to be sure all pieces are placed in the right direction using the safety pin as a guide. Use long, sharp, bent-handled dressmaker shears for cutting. Keep one hand flat on the edges of the pattern pieces and take long, smooth, slow and steady slashes. In order to cut **straight** edges, never cut all the way to the very tips.

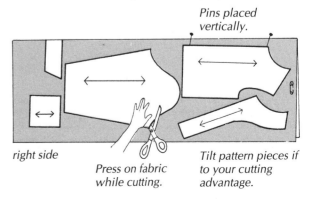

Pins placed vertically.

right side

Press on fabric while cutting.

Tilt pattern pieces if to your cutting advantage.

"dead" shears

Marking Tips

In general you can use your favorite marking method and tools to transfer construction marks to the wrong side of the garment pieces after cutting. Erasable marking pens, chalk quilting pencils and soft lead pencils as well as smooth-edged tracing wheel and tracing paper are all appropriate for transferring markings to the **wrong side. Test first** to make sure you can see the marks. Here are some of our favorite tips for marking speed and accuracy.

1. For **flat method** construction, extend the notches with pencil marks just inside the seamlines on pattern pieces **before** cutting away seam allowances for the overlap side of each seam. After cutting Ultrasuede, transfer the marks to the wrong side at the edges using chalk or lead pencil.

overlap side

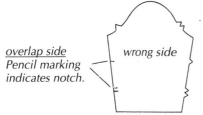

overlap side
Pencil marking indicates notch.
wrong side

2. Save time by snip marking notches, dots, and other construction symbols wherever possible. Just nip 1/8" into the seam allowances at the notch points.

snip
snip
snip
wrong side
snips on underlap
overlap

3. When cutting double layer, put pins vertically through dart points and other interior construction symbols (pocket locations, etc.). Lift the top layer of the Ultrasuede and mark both layers on the WRONG SIDE at the point where the pin penetrates the fabric. Connect dots with a ruler if you like.

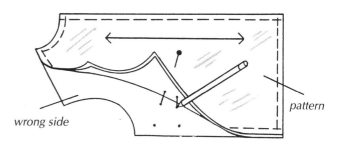

wrong side
pattern

4. After cutting and marking, stick a piece of transparent tape on the WRONG SIDE of each cut piece to avoid any mix-ups when sewing. Heaven forbid you should make up an Ultrasuede garment using the wrong side as the right side. (It's been known to happen!)

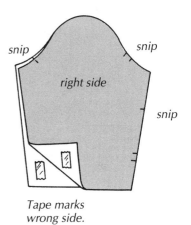

snip   *snip*
right side
snip
Tape marks wrong side.

CHAPTER 5:
Helpful Notions

Are they just gadgets or real conveniences??? Sometimes a great notion makes life very simple. Each of us has favorites we simply couldn't sew without! We've listed those that we find particularly helpful when sewing with Ultrasuede fabrics.

For Pinning and Cutting and Marking:

Pins—Fine, long pins with large, round glass heads are easiest to use on firm fabrics like Ultrasuede. We love the magnetized pin dish to hold them. (Grabbit or the Dritz Pin Catcher).

*magnetic
pin disk*

Cutting weights—Use them to hold patterns in place for pinless cutting! We like June Tailor's new non-slip decorator weights shaped like sewing tools. They fit easily into corners and curves on patterns and have easy-grip handles.

*June Tailor
pattern
weights*

Shears—Choose a pair of **very sharp** bent-handle dressmaker shears. A clean-cut edge is essential for flat construction methods so have your shears sharpened before cutting into Ultrasuede. Or treat yourself to a new pair! Marta hides her very best shears and uses them only for cutting Ultrasuede. Pati loves her 9" lightweight Henckel's dressmaker shears for speedier cutting.

*bent-
handled
dressmakers
shears*

Scissors—A pair of sharp, double-pointed 5" trimmers and/or a 3 1/2" embroidery scissors come in handy for trimming and for decorative cutwork.

scissors

Rotary cutter and mat—You might find it faster and easier to cut super straight lines with a rotary cutter and ruler. Barbara likes it for truing cut edges on pockets and flaps in flat construction. Work on a self-healing mat to protect your cutting surface and cut against a ruler for accuracy.

Marking tools—Use your favorite to mark construction symbols and darts on the WRONG SIDE. Pati prefers chalk or a lead pencil. Marta uses a white or yellow chalk pencil and Barbara likes water-soluble marking pens. Do not use standard writing or ball point pens; they usually run when you steam press or fuse.

*marking
chalk*

Buttonhole cutter—Use this extra-sharp cutter on its wooden block, for a clean, smooth cut.

*buttonhole
cutter*

For Hand and Machine Sewing

Sewing machine needles—Use a size 12 (80) needle for best results and to avoid making large holes in Ultrasuede. Choose the universal point Schmetz needle for European machines. **Do not** use leather needles; they make large holes and weaken the seams. When using thicker topstitching threads, use a larger needle, size 16 or 18 (100 or 110). Use a size 12 (80) Singer "Yellow Band" needle if you own a Singer machine. Its unique design prevents skipped stitches on Ultrasuede and other firmly finished fabrics.

Hand sewing needles—For the limited hand sewing you will do, choose a fine, size 10 sharp needle. A thimble is a necessity to protect your finger.

Thread—Choose a lightweight 100% polyester or a polyester core thread. We usually topstitch with regular thread, but for more obvious stitching, use one strand of polyester topstitching thread. **Always** do a stitching test sample through the same number of layers you will be using in the garment. Topstitching thread is good for sewing buttons on blazers and coats. Thread one shade darker than the fabric will appear lighter when sewn. A shade lighter gives a dressier, more elegant effect; a shade darker is sportier and a contrasting color even sportier.

Seam sealant—Use this clear, colorless liquid to secure thread knots. It won't wash or dry clean out. Our favorite is Dritz Fray Check™. Apply sparingly.

seam sealant

Basting tape—Use this 1/8"-wide, double-faced tape in place of pins or hand basting. It's a tremendous timesaver for zipper applications (page 43)! Some brands are water-soluble and wash out, but if you plan to dry clean the garment, remove the tape after stitching. If you stitch through basting tape by mistake, the needle gets "gummy" and skips stitches. Use rubbing alcohol to clean the residue from the needle.

> **PRO TIP:** Remove any tapes from Ultrasuede by pulling **with** the nap direction so you don't disturb or pull away any of the fibers.

Pressing Matters

Make construction pressing easier and more professional by using the right equipment. We wouldn't attempt to sew Ultrasuede fabrics without the following basic pressing equipment.

Steam iron—Look for a heavy iron with a large sole plate, lots of steam vents, and a "shot" or "surge-of-steam" feature. We prefer irons with large-capacity, water tanks since it takes lots of steam for fusing. We also like a nonstick soleplate surface when using fusible interfacings. You may pay more for an iron with all these features, but they will make pressing easier.

steam iron

> **QUICK TIP:** Your sewing iron **should not** have an automatic turn-off feature! It's a nuisance and a time-waster waiting for it to heat it up again.

Press—Several sewing machine companies offer these smaller versions of a dry cleaner's press for home sewers. We love to fuse interfacing on a press because it's so speedy. The pressing surface exerts 100 pounds of pressure for even, smooth fusing. Small pieces can be fused in one step, larger ones usually in two steps.

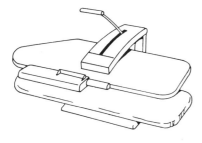

Cotton ironing board cover—Prevent shine and improve fusing with a cotton cover. June Tailor makes a nice one. Teflon-coated and aluminized finishes cause heat from the iron to bounce back and interfere with fusing. They also cause unwanted shine on the fabric surface, can make the fabric too hot, and even melt synthetics.

Pressing ham—a ham-shaped surface designed for pressing curved areas. Darts should be sewn to fit your curves. Press them over the same shaped curve on the ham.

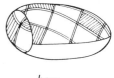

ham

Seam roll—a firmly stuffed, sausage shape that allows the garment to fall away from the seam edges so you can press along the stitching line and the seam edges won't make imprints in the garment. It also makes it easier to press seams in cylinders such as sleeves and pant legs.

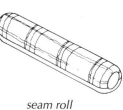

seam roll

Point presser/tailor's clapper—a wooden combination pressing tool. The point presser allows you to press enclosed seams open. You can even press all the way into the point of a collar!

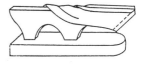

point presser/clapper combination

Use the heavier clapper portion to help flatten a seam after applying steam and heat with your iron. Since Ultrasuede is a synthetic, it only has a memory when cool. A clapper is important for getting a good flat press on conventional seams in Ultrasuede.

> **PRO TIP:** Fingers are a **free** pressing tool. Use them to lightly finger press a seam or dart in the right position **before** permanently pressing with the iron and tailor's clapper.

June Tailor board—a most versatile pressing tool with several "can't-live-without" surfaces shaped to fit a variety of curves, points and corners. It will sit or stand on your pressing surface in several different positions. Barbara wouldn't even consider doing conventional construction on an Ultrasuede garment without it. Press curved collar seams and jacket neckline seams open over the long curved edge. The small curve fits neatly into rounded collars and cuffs. We think it works best with the padded cover for the top surface, a **must** for Ultrasuede.

June Tailor board

Press cloths—Choose a sheer, see-through press cloth for fusing interfacing to protect the iron from picking up fusible residue. Both Dritz and June Tailor have nice ones. When top pressing is necessary on Ultrasuede, use a wool or heavy cotton flannel press cloth. Barbara's favorite is the June Tailor Steam 'N Shape ™ press cloth because its napped surface prevents shine and protects the nap.

Hot-iron cleaner—Remove fusible residue from the bottom of the iron with Dritz Iron-Off™.

The Ten Best Pressing Rules for Ultrasuede Fabrics

1. Remember Mom's number one rule—**press as you sew!**

2. Be sure you have a cotton cover on the ironing board or pressing surface. See page 24.

3. Use a **wool** setting and lots of steam.

4. Do most pressing from the **wrong side**, using a press cloth. For **limited top pressing** from the right side, **always, always, always** use a wool flannel or other napped-surface press cloth.

5. Press seams open over a seam roll to avoid seam imprints on the right side. Ultrasuede usually requires a second and third steam pressing after the first, followed by the tailor's clapper.

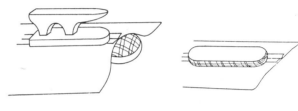

6. For nice, flat seams and edges that stay put, use the tailor's clapper. Work over a seam roll or place strips of paper under the seam allowances to prevent seam edge imprints on the right side. Marta also uses a seam roll as a clapper because it curves up and away from the seam edges, accomplishing the same pressing goals. Place the wool side (napped) of the seam roll against the Ultrasuede seam allowances after steaming with the iron.

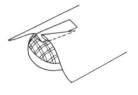

7. Use a pressing ham for darts and curved seams. Tuck a strip of paper under dart edge to prevent edge imprints on right side.

8. If seams won't press flat, use a press cloth dipped in a solution of 1 Tablespoon white vinegar to a cup of water.

9. If you get an iron imprint from too much pressure, quickly restore the nap with steam and by brushing with a soft clothes brush or a thick terry towel. **If the imprint is from too much heat, it's impossible to restore the nap on Ultrasuede.**

10. If you must rip stitches, remove needle holes with gentle steaming and brush with a soft brush.

PRO TIP: Pressing Ultrasuede takes **patience and care!!** Take your time and use the right equipment to avoid permanent shine, flattening the nap and iron imprints.

Suitable Shaping Fabrics

Ultrasuede garments need inner support and shaping just like everything else you sew. What you choose and where you put it in the garment depends on the desired effect as well as wearing comfort. You will need **interfacing** support in most garments and either a partial or complete **lining** as well.

Interfacing

Interfacings are a must in almost every garment. A collar has more body, a band won't pucker, and a machine buttonhole won't ripple if it's interfaced. Since Ultrasuede has quite a bit of body, it may seem like it doesn't need interfacing, but like other fabrics, it loses some of its body after several washings. We use lightweight to medium weight **fusible** interfacings because they are easy to apply and are very compatible with synthetic fabrics like Ultrasuede.

Where to Interface

1. Edges are subject to excessive wear. Use interfacing to provide strength and body and to prevent stretching at neckline, armhole and front edges. You may also choose to interface the hems (edges) in jackets and coats. Barbara does, Marta doesn't.

2. For better wear, interface high-stress areas—under buttons and buttonholes, for example.

3. Add shape and body to details—pockets, front bands and cuffs—for a positive fashion statement. They should look crisp, not droopy.

QUICK TIP: Marta suggests when making simple, loose-fitting vests from Ultrasuede, you can eliminate facings and interfacing since vests don't get as much wear. If you do choose to interface the edges of a single layer, unlined vest, use a fusible knit interfacing.

Don't Be Afraid of Fusible Interfacings!

We wouldn't use anything **but** fusible interfacings in Ultrasuede!! If you've been wary of fusibles because of the past poor performance of the old "iron-on" products, be wary no more. The first "iron-ons" were backed with flaky granules that fell off before you got them home! The fusing resins on the new generation of fusibles is evenly spread on the back of the fabric by either mechanical calendaring or a computer dot method.

When applied with the correct amount of steam, heat, pressure and time, today's fusible interfacings retain the shaping you want throughout the life of the garment. They can be machine washed and dried or dry-cleaned.

Now, Which Fusible?

The cardinal rule for choosing a fusible interfacing is **"always make a test sample first!"** Over the years, we've tested and tried every fusible interfacing available and we have some favorites for Ultrasuede, listed here. You may have others. We each have our own stash of favorite interfacings so that if we're in doubt about which would be best we can test several on the fabric, then make the decision. We don't recommend any of the heavyweight fuisbles for Ultrasuede.

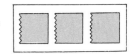

Cut one side of the interfacing with pinking shears to see if this makes the edge blend into the fabric better. Fuse.

Fusible weft-insertion interfacings combine the soft hand of a knit with the stability of a woven. Their base fabric is a warp-knitted fabric with yarns inserted (woven) into the knit loops in the crosswise (weft) direction. These interfacings are soft and drapable in the length yet quite stable in the width and have bias give like a woven interfacing. Even after washing a jacket 25 times, we've never had a bubbling problem with these interfacings!

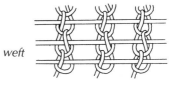

weft

warp

Brand names include: Armo R Weft (HTC), Suitmaker™ (Dritz), Tailor Fuse (J&R), Suit Maker (Staple) and Stylemaker 601 and 602 (J. N. Harper, Canada). We consider these medium weight to suitweight interfacings and like them especially for natural, tailored shaping.

Whisper Weft (HTC) and Sewer's Dream (J.N. Harper, Canada) are lighter versions for softer, more supple support.

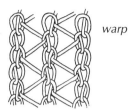

warp

Warp-insertion interfacings are similar to weft-insertion but the extra yarns are inserted vertically in a zigzag fashion, adding unique cross and lengthwise stretch for supple support. Soft 'N Silky (J & R) is the only one available and is similar in weight to Whisper Weft.

Vertical yarns "weave" in and out of the warp knit in a zigzag fashion, skipping over one row of knit loops.

Knit Fusibles are a bit softer and more flexible than weft- or warp-insertion interfacings. They stretch in the cross but not lengthwise direction. Use them as you would lightweight, nonwoven fusibles. We often use a patch of knit fusible interfacing at the elbow in Ultrasuede jacket sleeves to extend the wear. Brands include: Dritz Knit-Fuze™, Fusi-Knit from HTC, Stacy® Easy Knit® from Pellon, Quick Knit by J & R, and French Fuse from Staple.

Preshrink Fusible Interfacings

Not everyone agrees on this subject, but we recommend preshrinking all interfacings, including fusibles. Many are labeled "preshrunk," but that doesn't necessarily mean "Will not shrink." Most fabrics, including interfacings, are wrapped tautly on bolts, so relaxation shrinkage can occur during steaming and laundering. The heat of the iron can cause shrinkage, too. Why take the chance that your interfacing will bubble or come unfused altogether? Here's how to preshrink them:

1. Place loosely folded interfacing yardage in a basin of **hot** tap water. It's OK—it takes at least 300° F to activate the fusing agents. Soak 20 to 30 minutes. Do not agitate, wad up or wring the interfacing. **Don't preshrink fusibles in the washing machine!** The abrasion can cause the adhesive resin to flake off.

2. Drain the water and gently pat the interfacing to remove excess water. Roll it in a towel, then hang the interfacing over a towel rod to dry. Lay knit interfacings flat to dry. **Do not dry in the dryer!**

3. Even after preshrinking in hot water, some fusibles may shrink more from the steam and heat of the iron. To be **safe**, steam-shrink these interfacings after cutting and just before fusing by holding the iron an inch above the interfacing and steaming for five seconds. Move the iron over and repeat until you've steamed the entire piece. Sometimes you can see the interfacing draw up, but this will not affect the finished garment. After steaming, use your hands to smooth out the interfacing if necessary, then fuse.

How to Fuse

After you've chosen the best fusible(s) for your Ultrasuede garment, proper fusing is essential. **Always** read the manufacturer's instructions. They may change slightly when a product is improved.

Preheat iron to wool setting, but **remember:** home iron temperatures can vary a great deal. You may need a higher or lower setting or to adjust the number of seconds you hold the iron in one spot.

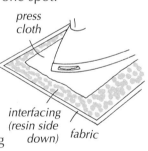

press cloth

interfacing (resin side down)

fabric

Even moisture is critical to bonding. Use an **evenly** damp, see-through press cloth. Be careful not to get it too wet. Water bubbles that form between the fusible and fabric will remain unfused, causing noticeable dimpling or bubbling on the fabric surface when water evaporates.

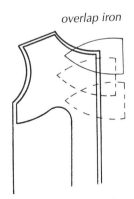

overlap iron

Time the fusing. Most fusibles require 10 to 15 seconds all over. Clock the time each time you put the iron down. **To avoid creating an iron imprint on Ultrasuede,** fuse **only** 4 to 5 seconds in one spot, lift the iron. Move to a new spot in the same general location, put iron down overlapping last location; fuse. Continue this until area is completely fused, a total of 10-15 seconds.

Pressure creates a firm bond. Press down firmly on the iron as you fuse. To increase the pressure, lower your ironing board and really lean on the iron. But be careful to put equal pressure on the heel and toe of the iron.

Four Tips for Successful Fusing

If you don't do a good job of fusing, fusible interfacings can pull away from the fabric during laundering. **Then** the problem is **impossible** to fix. Follow these tips for successful fusing.

1. Position the interfacing, resin side down and **steam-shrink** it. See page 27.

2. **Always use a press cloth** to protect the iron and any exposed edges of the fashion fabric.

3. **Overlap iron positions** as you move to a new fusing location so you don't miss a spot. Marta suggests working from the top down, always overlapping as you go.

4. Always **allow the fused piece to cool** before you move it. After cooling, check adhesion by trying to lift one edge of the interfacing. If necessary, fuse for an additional 5 to 10 seconds.

How to Use a Press for Speedy Fusing

Cut fusing time in half with a press. Since large garment sections won't fit entirely on the bed of the press, follow these steps for the best fuse.

1. Working on a flat surface, position the interfacing on the garment and steam-shrink using an iron as described on page 27.

2. Steam-baste the interfacing to the garment section by touching the iron to the pieces for one second in several different spots.

3. Place the steam-basted unit in the press, interfacing side up with a press cloth on top. Mist liberally with water. Lower the press and fuse the entire section at once. Repeat with any remaining unfused section of the piece. Allow to cool.

Lining

A lining is assembled separately and "finishes" the inside of a garment. It covers inner construction—welt pockets, shoulder pads, and interfacing—and makes the garment easier to slide on over other clothing. Since Ultrasuede is not at all slippery, we recommend lining or partially lining most Ultrasuede garments. It's difficult to slip into a jacket when your sweater is sticking to the sleeves. And a skirt that "climbs" up your legs is uncomfortable and unsightly!

What to line:

1. Tailored coats and jackets need a lining to cover inner construction. Unlined casual jackets and loose-fitting coats will be easier to wear if the sleeves are lined. See page 101 for partial lining how-tos.

2. Fitted Ultrasuede skirts need a lining if you don't want to wear a slip. If you don't like the rustling sound of some lining fabrics, try an anti-static nylon tricot.

3. Lining is optional in vests. You may want to line more fitted styles with tailored welt pockets but not line looser ones.

4. Marta likes light-colored linings for handbags, so you can see inside them. Cotton or cotton/poly blends are easy-sew, wear better and things don't slide around inside the finished bag.

Some things to consider when choosing a lining:

1. Make a fashion statement in an Ultrasuede garment. Choose a super print or a contrasting color lining. You'll get lots of attention when your jacket is draped over a chair and will have fun wearing the "surprise" inside.

2. Select a lining with the same features as Ultrasuede (machine washable and dryable, no pressing necessary, very durable). Look for light- to medium weight woven polyester fabrics with a smooth, slick surface.

3. Dyed-to-match lining fabrics are often available for Ultrasuede. We also like polyester crepe de chines and faille for coat and jacket linings. Balisse, Palazzio and Sensensual are marketed by the Ultrasuede Group to coordinate with Ultrasuede fabrics.

CHAPTER 8:
Make It Fit!

Take time to check your body measurements **before** purchasing your pattern. Bodies change, even when there is no weight change. Buying the right pattern size gives you confidence to cut into Ultrasuede!

For blouses, jackets, coats and dresses: Since patterns are drafted for the average B-cup bra size, if you're a DD and you buy according to your bust measurement, your pattern will be too large in the neckline and shoulders. For a better fit:

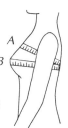

Take **TWO** measurements, your chest or "high bust" (A) and full bust (B). If the difference between these two is 2 1/2" or more, substitute the "high bust" for bust on measurement chart. If pattern is then too small in the bust, adjust for a full bust, page 31.

As a general rule, if you are between sizes, **choose the smaller size**. Patterns have enough wearing ease to fit up to the next size. For example, Barbara measures 33 3/4" and sews with a size 10. A 12 is too large in the shoulders and neckline.

Size	6	8	10	12	14	16	18	20	22	24
Bust	30¹/₂	31¹/₂	32¹/₂	34	36	38	40	42	44	46
Waist	23	24	25	26¹/₂	28	30	32	34	37	39
Hip	32¹/₂	33¹/₂	34¹/₂	36	38	40	42	44	46	48
Back Waist Length	15¹/₂	15³/₄	16	16¹/₄	16¹/₂	16³/₄	17	17¹/₄	17³/₈	17¹/₂

For skirts and pants: Use full hip measurement for fitted skirts or pants and adjust waistline to fit. For full skirt and **very full-cut** pant designs, purchase pattern by your waistline measurement since that's the only place these styles touch your body.

So What's This Thing Called Ease?

Patterns have two types of ease: **wearing ease,** so you can move comfortably and **design ease** for the desired fashion look. Some close-to-the-body styles may have less than the minimum wearing ease normally allowed. Flat pattern measuring, above, is the only way you can really tell how much ease your pattern has and how it will fit your body.

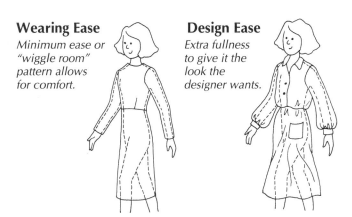

Wearing Ease
Minimum ease or "wiggle room" pattern allows for comfort.

Design Ease
Extra fullness to give it the look the designer wants.

Allow for enough ease to move comfortably. Check the chart for **minimum wearing ease** recommended for Ultrasuede garments; compare to your pattern's flat pattern measurements. Make fitting changes **before you cut!** Always cut garments with **at least** minimum wearing ease beyond your body measurements and you'll eliminate most fitting disasters.

Minimum Wearing Ease

	Bust	Waist	Hip	Sleeve
Dresses	2¹/₂"	2¹/₂"	2¹/₂"	2¹/₂"
Jackets	4"	–	4"	4¹/₂"
Coats	5"	–	5"	5¹/₂"
Fitted Skirts	–	1"	2"	–
Trousers	–	1"	3"	–
Jeans	–	2"	0"	–

Flat pattern measure at critical fit points—bust, upper arm, waist, high hip, full hipline. Compare to yours. Some measurements are printed on the tissue but your full hip may not be in the same place as the full hip on the pattern! Make sure the pattern is large enough to fit you **plus** at least minumum wearing ease, above.

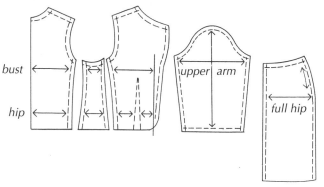

Fit Before You Cut!

When sewing an Ultrasuede garment with flat method construction, you cut away one seam allowance in each seam so what you cut is what you get! Only minor fitting changes are possible after cutting.

Tissue fit first to check the style and spot needed length and width adjustments. Cut away excess tissue; press pattern with warm, dry iron. Pin in darts, turn and pin up hems; pin together with pins on the seamlines, points down so you don't get poked. Clip armhole and neck curves to the seamline about every inch so tissue won't tear. Try on. Tuck shoulder pads in place if needed. Pin center front and back to your clothes at center front and back. Check fit, working from top down so you don't miss anything. Check sleeve, bodice, skirt and pant lengths. See "Common Fitting Adjustments" on page 31.

Make a test garment first if you have many pattern adjustments or design changes to make. Use a medium-weight, nonwoven interfacing; it will hang like Ultrasuede for a good idea of how your pattern will look and fit. Pin together and check the fit as directed for actual garment, below. Take test garment apart to use for a trial layout to determine needed yardage (page 10).

Use a pattern you have sewn before—a smart move only **if** you worked out any fitting changes **and** marked them on your pattern. Check the fit of the previous garment, wearing the same garments and undergarments you will wear with your finished Ultrasuede garment.

Check the Fit After You Cut and Before You Stitch

Fit as you sew, making any necessary adjustments as you go. Who can afford a $100+ **"surprise"** that doesn't fit?!

1. Pin garment together as you will sew it. For **conventional method,** pin seams and darts WRONG SIDES together.

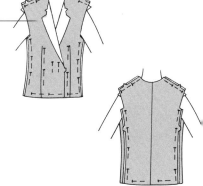

For **flat method,** lap raw edges to seamlines on the RIGHT SIDE with pins parallel to cut edges. Pin darts as for conventional method. (Pin holes will steam out later.)

Try on garment and re-pin seams and darts until you're happy with the fit.

2. Remove garment. For **conventional construction:** open seams; run tailor's chalk or a marking pencil along pins to mark final seamlines.

For flat construction: mark every underlap edge onto the WRONG SIDE of the corresponding piece to show where to lap and steam-baste seams. Mark dart locations as for conventional construction, above.

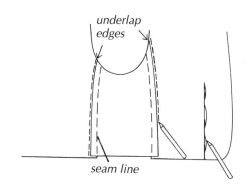

underlap edges

seam line

Common Fitting Adjustments

Check for these adjustments while tissue fitting and correct in the pattern tissue **before** cutting.

Full Bustline Adjustment—A gaping front armhole and pulls across the bustline mean you need this ajustment. If you bought your pattern using the high bust measurement (page 29) and you are a C cup or larger, you now need to give your bustline more room by increasing the size of the pattern's existing darts.

1. Try on pattern and mark bust point (apex) with soft tip pen. Draw line A through dart to apex. If pattern has no dart, draw line A where you'd like one.

2. Draw line B from armhole notch to apex and line C from apex to bottom of pattern, (through the center of any existing dart). Add line D perpendicular to line C between waistline and bottom edge.

3. Cut on C to apex, continuing on B to, **but not through**, armhole. Cut along A to, but not through apex. At arrow spread: 1/2" for C Cup; 3/4" for D; 1 1/4" or more for DD cup.

4. Cut on D and drop until hems are even. Add tissue. Redraw dart to point to the apex. **Extend front vertical darts to the hemline.**

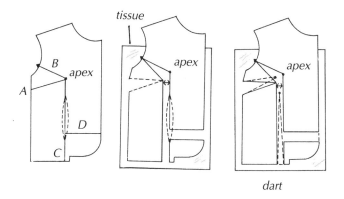

tissue *apex* *apex* *apex*
B *apex* A D C *dart*

FIT TIP: If you prefer no dart, are fuller in **both** the chest and upper arm and just need a little extra room, try adding extra fullness to the sleeve and bodice front and back. Taper to nothing 6" to 8" below the armhole.

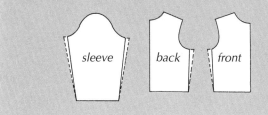

sleeve *back* *front*

Full Hipline—To increase the hipline in a jacket, add equally to front, back and side panel, beginning at armhole. Divide amount you need to add by the total number of side seam allowances; in this case 4 on each side=8. Add that amount to each side at full hip when you cut.

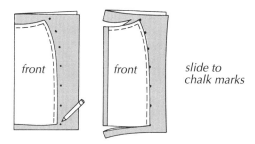

back *front*

To increase the hipline in a straight skirt: Divide the total amount you need by 4 seam allowances and chalk mark the amount you need to add at the sides on the fabric. Cut all but the side seams and slide the pattern pieces to chalk marks. Cut side seams. Slide pattern back to mark darts or tucks.

front *front* *slide to chalk marks*

If the waistline is now too large, sew deeper side seams to fit your shape. Do not add or sew deeper darts—they will only "pooch out," especially in Ultrasuede!

Sway Back Or Straight Back—Adjust for this if side seams swing forward and the hem always touches your legs in back. This is very common and **must be corrected before cutting.**

Shorten at center back with a tuck at or above waistline that makes center back hang straight. Tuck tapers to nothing at side seam. Straighten center back and grainline. For skirt, pull up at center back until side seams hang straight. Sew waistband at new **lower** seamline at center back, tapering back to normal waistline at side seams.

Other adjustments including full upper arm and wide back are covered in the fitting section in **"Mother Pletsch's Painless Sewing."** See page 127.

CHAPTER 9:
Stitching Tips for Ultrasuede

A longer-than-average stitch length is usually best for stitching conventional seams and for edge- or topstitching on Ultrasuede. Shorter stitch lengths can weaken the seams. The appearance of 8 to 10 stitches per inch is desirable. Since Ultrasuede is a somewhat spongy, textured fabric it will take up some of the stitch length just by passing through the fabric. Do a test sample through the same fabric layers you will be stitching and judge the stitch length by the appearance, not by the stitch length number on the machine.

New sewing machines and notions make it easier than ever to sew on Ultrasuede. On some older machines you may find it has a tendency to stick to the presser foot, preventing normal feeding and resulting in irregular stitch lengths, puckered seams and seam slippage. Do a stitching test sample on scraps. If you have any of these problems, try one of these special presser feet. Check with your sewing machine dealer.

Teflon foot—has a non-stick, coated sole so it glides over the fabric for even feeding.

Roller foot— "rolls" along the fabric instead of sliding as the normal presser foot does.

Even-feed or "walking foot"— has built-in feed dogs so it "walks" on top of the fabric in step with the machine's feed dogs beneath the fabric.

You can also correct stitching problems with **taut sewing.** Pull equally on the fabric in front of and behind the needle as you sew. **Do not stretch the fabric,** just pull taut, as if fabric is being held in an embroidery hoop, so it feeds evenly.

When doing **multiple rows** of stitching for decorative work through two layers or when stitching on bands and cuffs, sew all rows in the same direction to avoid creeping and wrinkling between rows. Steam-basting layers together with strips of fusible web before stitching helps just as steam-basting lapped seams for flat construction prevents rippling or wrinkling when doing both edgestitching and topstitching.

Skipped Stitches???

1. Try a new needle!

2. Try "taut sewing." (See above).

3. Replace the zigzag plate with a straight-stitch needle plate for added support around the needle. (Check with your dealer.) Or, cover the needle slot of the zigzag plate with masking tape.

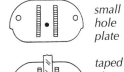

small hole plate

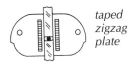

taped zigzag plate

4. The machine may balk and skip stitches when stitching over thick seam intersections. Tuck a small piece of cardboard or a folded scrap of Ultrasuede under back end of presser foot to level it with the thicker seam. Stitch over the "hump" and remove the cardboard.

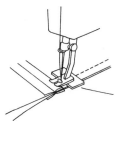

5. Sometimes just washing the fabric helps.

Ripping

Don't panic! Needle holes will show when you rip out stitches in Ultrasuede but will seal up again with steam pressing. If a hole is particularly stubborn, hold the steam iron 1" away from the surface and steam well; then brush the area immediately with a small, soft-bristled brush. Repeat if necessary.

When ripping lapped seams, **do not reheat steam-basted seams.** It only makes them more difficult to separate. Simply remove stitching, then use rubbing alcohol to soften and remove fusible web instead.

Terrific Edgestitching and Topstitching

Stitching accuracy is the key to a beautifully sewn Ultrasuede garment. Both conventional and flat method construction require lots of edge- and/or topstitching. Technically, topstitching is any stitching done on the top of the garment. We like to differentiate between edgestitching and topstitching.

In **flat method** construction you only need to do edgestitching which results in a dressier look. Edgestitching **plus** topstitching, usually spaced 1/4" away from the edgestitching, creates a sportier look. In **conventional method** construction, one row of topstitching spaced 1/4" from the edge or seamline is most common. It adds a decorative touch while holding edges firmly in place.

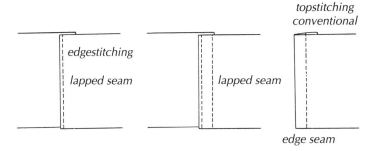

topstitching conventional

edgestitching

lapped seam

lapped seam

edge seam

Easier Edgestitching and Topstitching

You can often use the **inside edge** of the **right toe** of the presser foot as a guide for even edgestitching. If that's not quite close enough to the edge to suit you, try moving the needle position on zigzag machines slightly to the **right.** On some machines, you can use the blind hem or edgestitch foot for even edgestitching. Check your machine manual.

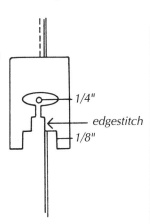

1/4"

edgestitch

1/8"

Three Ways to Do Straight and Even Topstitching

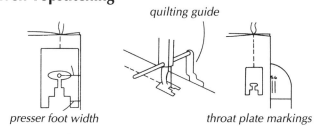

quilting guide

presser foot width

throat plate markings

QUICK TIP: If your presser foot doesn't measure 1/4" from the needle hole to the outside edge, change the standard and use what your presser foot does measure as a topstitching guide. Some measure almost 3/8". Or, move needle position.

Perfect Pivots

To keep your machine from "eating" a corner when you pivot, sew to the corner, stopping to hand wheel the needle into the fabric at the corner so it completes the stitch, connecting with the bobbin thread and it's on its way **up** again. Then pivot and continue stitching. Since the needle is on its way out of the fabric, it won't push the corner down into the machine and you won't lose the stitch at the corner.

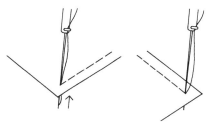

Topstitch a blazer notch as shown. Pivot at the gorge line, "stitch in the ditch" or well of the seam for 2-3 stitches. Turn the corner and continue stitching.

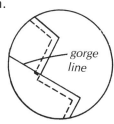

gorge line

PRO TIP: A blazer lapel folds to the outside, so if using heavier topstitching thread, you will need to break the stitching at the roll line. Beginning at the end of the roll line, stitch with the facing and upper collar facing you. Below the roll line, stitch with the front of the jacket facing you. Pull threads to the inside between the facing and front layers, tie a dressmaker's knot (overhand). Dab with Fray Check for extra hold.

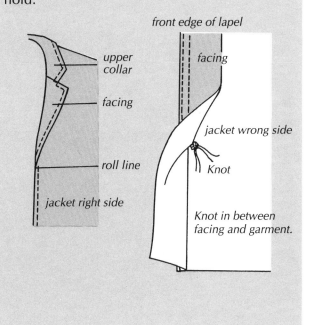

front edge of lapel

upper collar

facing

facing

roll line

jacket wrong side

Knot

jacket right side

Knot in between facing and garment.

CHAPTER 10

Start With Something Easy–Belts, Vests and Bags

If you're a little wary of tackling a skirt or jacket for your first Ultrasuede sewing project, start with something smaller. It won't take much time or money to make a belt, a simple vest, or a little clutch bag and you'll gain the **confidence to cut** into your first small piece of Ultrasuede. Overcome that fear and the sewing is easy. Small projects give you a chance to practice steam-basting and stitching techniques and to get acquainted with how the fabric handles. And, we know you'll want to keep on sewing with this marvelous fabric after your first experience because of it's versatility and the creative doors it can open.

In fact, you can get quite creative with simple sewing projects—especially if you've saved your scraps from larger Ultrasuede projects. Don't ever throw anything but the tiniest of scraps away. We spotted a great piece of wearable art in a trendy New York City gallery with front panels embellished with confetti-like pieces of suede fused, then stitched in place. A little machine stitchery and beading were added for interest. Your Ultrasuede scrapbox is a real treasure trove!

Cut-and-Go and Sew-and-Go Belts

Many Ultrasuede belts are simply cut-and-go, others require only a little stitching and still others a little creativity, a pretty buckle and the belt-maker's best friend—a little hook and loop tape such as Velcro®.

For your first belt, cut a 1/8 yard-wide strip of Ultrasuede from selvage to selvage. That will make a 4 1/2"x 46" strip to wrap and tie around your waist and you'll save at least $12. Ultrasuede and real suede strip belts cost $18 to $25 in better boutiques!! We can't think of a better incentive to take the first cut. Use a rotary cutter and mat for this simple belt, if you prefer and shape the ends for added interest.

Or cut the strip first, then use a scalloping or pinking shears all around, barely trimming the straight edge away.

Measure your waistline and shape the strip where it will tie in the center, rounding the ends, too. Then "finish" the edges all around with a scalloping stitch on the machine and trim out the scallop points with a very sharp embroidery scissors. Because Ultrasuede stretches on the crosswise, you may get some rippling when you use decorative stitches. That's OK. It adds interest.

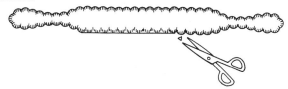

Try stacking two strips of varying widths and colors for a multicolor look. Steam-baste and stitch them together—or simply make a variety of strips in different colors and widths to stack and tie interchangeably, matching them to what you're wearing. You can twist strips together, too.

Cut two shorter strips from the same or different colors, rounding the ends. Overlap ends at the center back, fuse, then edgestitch together.

Create a belt strip of the desired width with overlapping blocks of color—a great scrapbox project. Back with a straight strip of one color, steam-baste the layers, WRONG SIDES together, and edgestitch.

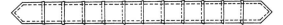

For belts with buckles, cut an Ultrasuede strip 3"x 36" (or longer if you need it). Easestitch one end, draw up the stitching and stitch to a 1"x 1 1/2" Velcro® strip. Pull the Velcro end through half of a pretty buckle and secure with the other half of Velcro sewn to the wrong side of the belt by hand or machine.

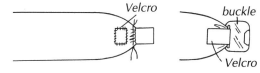

Velcro   *buckle*   *Velcro*

Pull the remaining end of the suede through the other half of the buckle and try on to determine how long to make the finished belt. Then easestitch, apply Velcro tab and complete the belt. Now you can use that expensive buckle on other similar suede belts.

For belts with more body, cut two identical strips and a strip of fusible web the length you want and about 1/4" wider than the desired finished width. Fuse, trim to the desired width and shape, and edgestitch or decoratively stitch as you wish.

Then go a step further. Stack contrasting colors in interesting shapes, steam-baste and edgestitch together. Fuse to another layer of Ultrasuede and edgestitch. Add a beautiful buckle with Velcro tabs or make hidden closures with hooks and eyes or Velcro for front or back opening belts. Simply gorgeous belts and real moneysavers!

For even more body, wrap and fuse a strip of Ultrasuede around a piece of Armoflexxx or Ban-Roll monofilament nylon waistband interfacing, cut to fit your waist measurement plus 3". Cut the suede twice the width of the interfacing plus 1/4". Center and fuse the interfacing on the wrong side of the suede. Wrap the long edges to the back side of the interfacing and fuse with additional strips of fusible web, with 1/4" of suede overlapping the remaining raw edge for a neat finish. Slip the ends through the bars of a clasp-style buckle, adjust to fit your waist and machine stitch or secure with strips of Velcro as shown above if you want to use the buckle on other belts.

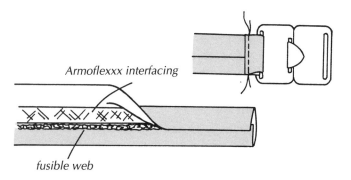

Armoflexxx interfacing

fusible web

Use decorative stitching to embellish the suede first. Double-needle pintucking is very effective. Or, use decorative threads in the upper and lower loopers to add a pretty edge-finish to your Ultrasuede tie belts.

twin needle topstiching

Making Ultrasuede belts is quick and easy and there are no creative limits. If you use your scraps, they're FREE! Most take 1/8 yard or less so the investment is minimal if you must purchase the materials—still a bargain when you check out belt prices in boutiques. What better incentive to make your own belts! We know you could build a thriving business just making wonderful Ultrasuede belts to sell at bazaars and craft shows.

Start collecting belt ideas from mail-order catalogs and fashion magazines. Barbara makes sketches of spendy or interesting belts when she's out snoop shopping. Her belt file is bulging with more ideas than she'll probably ever be able to make up or wear. But then, her Christmas gift list is a long one so she can make a good stab at it! For starters, see our belt collection on pages 78 and 79.

Ultra Easy Vests

If you're ready to graduate to an easy Ultrasuede garment, make a simple vest or pullover tabard using flat construction. You'll get almost instant gratification from minimal yardage and a few minutes of sewing.

Using a standard, loosely fitting vest pattern, lap and steam-baste the fronts over the back at the shoulders and side seams and edgestitch. Cut and add front and neckline facings only if you want buttons and buttonholes. (Armhole and hem facings are optional and only need to be 5/8"-wide.) Steam-baste and edgestitch facings in place. Edgestitch the raw hemline edge if desired. Make stitch and slash buttonholes (page 82).

To save yardage, cut vest fronts from Ultrasuede and the back from lining fabric. Construct the back following the pattern guidesheet, then serge raw edges at the back shoulder and underarm seams. Lap, steam-baste and edgestitch the fronts to the back.

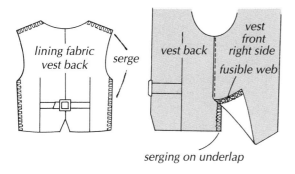

serging on underlap

Cut a simple pullover vest using a sweatshirt pattern. Change the neck to a V-neckline and scallop with scalloping shears or draw and cut larger scallop shapes freehand if desired. Lap, steam-baste, and stitch the fronts over the back at shoulders and side seams.

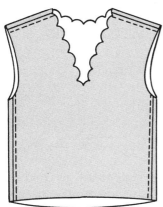

Sew Wonderful Bags and Totes

Marta is a firm believer in making your own handbags, totes and clutches from Ultrasuede. "Dollar for dollar," she says, "they're probably the best investment you can make when you compare the costs to ready-made bags of similar quality."

Soft clutches, envelope-style bags and sturdy totes are simple to sew and can become a focus for creative treatments, too. Kits and hardware for beautiful, professional-looking bags are available from notions mail-order sources. Most take less than an hour to sew, require minimal yardage and the frames can be removed easily so you can wash your suede bags when they really need it.

Sunglasses Case

Fold a 7" square of Ultrasuede in half. Steam-baste and edgestitch the bottom and side edges together. Try a decorative stitch at the edges. Or, use your serger. Use a decorative thread in the upper and lower looper. Finish one edge of the square with a wide, balanced stitch. Fold in half, WRONG SIDES TOGETHER, and serge the bottom and sides to finish. Knot the thread tails securely; thread the ends through the eye of a large needle and bury them between the fabric layers.

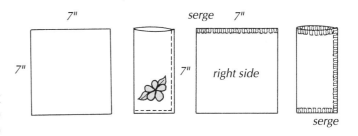

Tuck a square of Ultrasuede inside the case for cleaning your glasses. It's soft and won't scratch the lenses.

For an even sturdier, **padded case,** cut a 7 1/2" square of Ultrasuede and a 7"x7 1/2" square of fusible web, polyester fleece, and fusible knit interfacing. Fuse interfacing to one side of the fleece. Then use fusbile web to fuse Ultrasuede to the other side. Machine quilt the padded square if desired. Turn under the extra 1/2" of Ultrasuede, and stitch close to the raw edge. Then fold in half lengthwise with the suede inside and stitch or serge 1/2" from the bottom and side. Turn right side out.

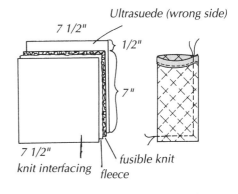

NOTE: Spring closures for eyeglass cases are available from some notions mail-order catalogs.

Easy Foldover Clutch Bag

1. Cut two 9"x12" Ultrasuede rectangles. For added body, fuse a slightly smaller rectangle of weft-insertion or fusible knit interfacing to the WRONG SIDE of one of the rectangles.

2. Mark two 1/4"x 7" boxes on the remaining rectangle as shown. Cut out carefully. Steam-baste a 7" zipper under each opening. Or use basting tape to hold the zippers in place. Edgestitch around each opening using a zipper foot.

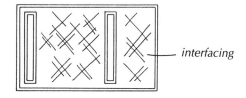

3. With WRONG SIDES facing, stitch the two bag sections together in the center to create two pockets and a natural foldline. Edgestitch bag to finish. For a more decorative look, add decorative topstitching or an applique to the outside piece before stitching the layers together.

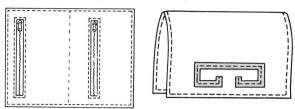

It's easy to change the dimensions of the rectangles and zippers for a larger bag. Interface both rectangles for extra body in larger bags. Before fusing interfacing in place, make zipper cutouts in the interfacing slightly larger than in the suede so the interfacing won't show at the cut edges around the zipper.

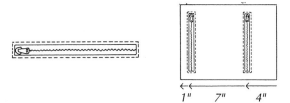

Consider padding and quilting the outer layer of the bag before stitching as shown for the eyeglasses case on page 37. Use conventional seaming to sew the two layers together, **leaving a zipper open** so you can turn the bag right side out. After turning right side out, stitch through the center of the bag and topstitch 1/4" from the outer edges if desired.

Marta's 1/4-Yard Bag

Make one of Marta's handy little shoulder bags from:
1/4 yard each of Ultrasuede and a woven lining fabric;
1/2 yard fusible web;
1/4 yard polyester fleece;
5"x11 1/2" piece of fusible interfacing; 2 Velcro dot closures

1. Cut all bag pieces from the Ultrasuede as shown. Cut matching pieces from the fusible web. Cut the bag front and back from fleece. Cut the front, back and pocket from lining.

shoulder strap 1"x25"			
			flap 4 1/2"x10 1/2"
front 8"x11 1/2"	back 8"x11 1/2"	outside pocket 5"x11 1/2"	flap facing 4 1/2"x10 1/2"

2. Fold strap in half lengthwise, WRONG SIDES facing. Fuse layers together and edgestitch. Sandwich fusible web between bag front and fleece; fuse. Repeat with back pieces. Fuse interfacing to WRONG SIDE of the pocket.

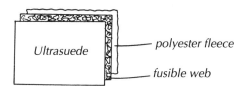

Ultrasuede — polyester fleece — fusible web

3. Stitch hook half of Velcro dot closure to RIGHT SIDE of flap facing at two corners. Fuse the flap and flap facing together, WRONG SIDES facing. Edgestitch two short edges and one long edge of flap, rounding the corners. Trim.

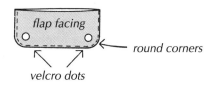

flap facing — round corners — velcro dots

4. Stitch pocket lining to one long edge of pocket, RIGHT SIDES TOGETHER in a 1/4"-wide seam. Turn, press and edgestitch. Pin to bag front with side and bottom edges matching.

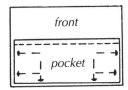

front

pocket

5. With RIGHT SIDES facing, stitch bag front to bag back at sides and bottom in 1/2"-wide seam. Pinch the seams so side seams line up with bottom seam to form a corner triangle. Stitch across triangle 1/2" from point. Stitch close to first stitching; trim. Turn bag right side out.

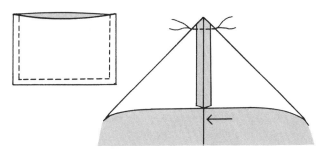

DESIGNER TIP: The farther in you stitch from the triangle point the wider the sides and bottom of the finished bag will be.

side view

6. Center and pin the flap to bag back with long edges matching. Center and pin strap ends over side seams.

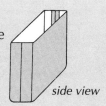

flap

back

7. Stitch bag front and back lining together at sides and bottom; leave 5" opening in bottom. Pinch and stitch corners as for bag. Slip bag into lining, RIGHT SIDES TOGETHER. Stitch top edges together in 1/4"-wide seam. Turn right side out through lining opening. Turn in seam allowances at bottom opening; edgestitch to finish. Tuck lining into bag.

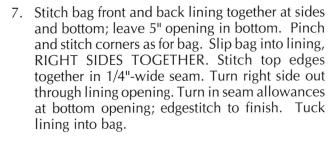

lining

wrong side

5" opening

9. Sew Velcro dot closures to front pocket to match dots on underside of flap.

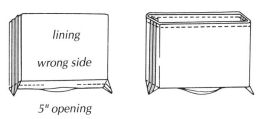

DESIGNER TIP: Add trim or decorative appliques to the bag flap and the bag back before assembling the pieces. Or, embellish the pieces with machine embroidery, cutwork or quilting first. See page 119 for other creative ideas for Ultrasuede. You can also restyle the flap and eliminate the strap to make this into a clutch bag. Try it in black and add a beaded, glittery applique for evening!

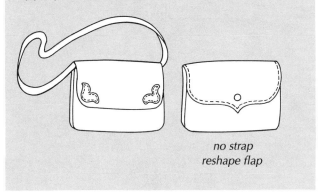

no strap
reshape flap

Marta's Terrific Tote

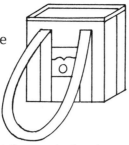

Marta designed and made an Ultrasuede tote like this over nine years ago and it's still in great shape!

You will need: 1/2 yard Ultrasuede for the tote and two pocket squares; 1/4 yard contrasting Ultrasuede for straps and pocket appliques; 1/2 yard of firmly woven cotton or cotton/poly fabric for the lining; 120" of 1"-wide Armoflexxx or Ban Rol waistband interfacing; and two 18" squares each of fusible web and polyester fleece.

1. Cut two 18" squares from Ultrasuede and lining fabric. Set lining pieces aside. Fuse fleece to WRONG SIDE of each Ultrasuede square.

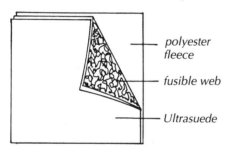

- polyester fleece
- fusible web
- Ultrasuede

2. Stitch Ultrasuede squares, RIGHT SIDES TOGETHER, in a 1/4" seam. Press seam open. Stitch 1/8" from seamline on each side of seam. Repeat with lining squares.

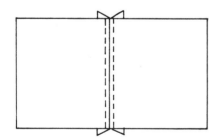

3. Cut one or two 9"x9" pockets as desired. Cut applique shapes from contrasting Ultrasuede scraps. Steam-baste in place on the pocket and edgestitch.

4. Center and steam-baste completed pockets on tote front (and back) with bottom edge 6" from seamline. Edgestitch bottom of pocket to tote.

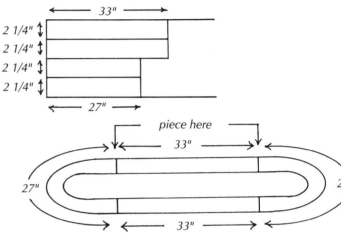

6"

6"

5. For continuous strap, cut and piece a 2 1/4"x120" strip of contrasting Ultrasuede as shown.

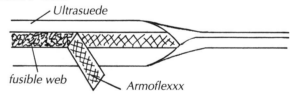

6. Center and fuse Armoflexxx to WRONG SIDE of each strap. Wrap raw edges of Ultrasuede around Armoflexxx and fuse with additional strips of fusible web.

Ultrasuede

fusible web   Armoflexxx

7. Position strap on bag with the piecing seams 1 1/4" from the top edges of the front and back pieces. Lap the inner edge of strap over outer edges of pockets 1/4". Steam-baste in place, stopping at the strap piecing seams.

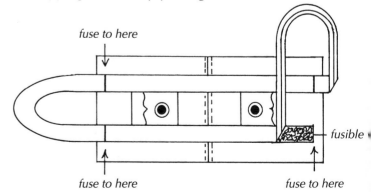

fuse to here

fuse to here   fuse to here

fusible

8. Edgestitch strap to tote, pivoting at piecing seams. Reinforce at upper edges by stitching in an "X" as shown.

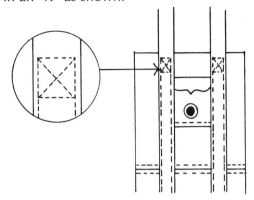

9. Fold tote in half, RIGHT SIDES together, and stitch side seams in 1/2"-wide seams. Press seams open. Repeat with lining.

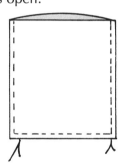

DESIGNER TIP: Before stitching side seams in lining, add an inside pocket if you wish.

inside pocket

10. Pinch seams so side seams line up with bottom seam to form corner triangles. Stitch across triangle 3 " from point. Trim away excess. Turn right side out. Pinch and stitch lining seams the same way.

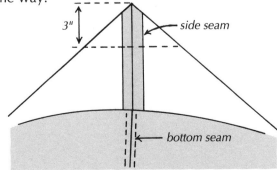

3"

side seam

bottom seam

11. Fold and edgestitch tote bottom from corner to corner as shown.

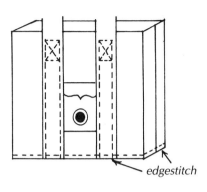

edgestitch

12. Tuck completed lining into Ultrasuede tote, WRONG SIDES together. Bind top of tote with 1 1/2"-wide strips of matching or contrasting Ultrasuede cut on crosswise grain. With RIGHT SIDES TOGETHER, stitch binding to tote in 3/8"-wide seam. Wrap binding around raw edge, steam press lightly and stitch in the well (ditch) of seam to catch binding in place. Trim binding close to stitching.

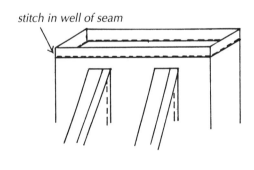

stitch in well of seam

13. For stability and support in the bottom of the tote, cut a rectangle of 1/4"-thick foam board (available at art supply or frame shops) or heavy corrugated cardboard. Measure and cut for a **tight fit** in bottom of tote. Cover with excess lining fabric and slip into tote. Remove for laundering.

CHAPTER 11:
Darts

Darts control fullness and shape a flat piece of fabric to your body curves. They require special handling in firm fabrics like Ultrasuede. You will need darts in many Ultrasuede garments to create some shaping but it's best to avoid them in the front of Ultrasuede skirts as they have a tendency to pucker at the point, no matter how they're stitched and pressed.

Convert front darts to soft ease in fitted skirts. Adjust the ease during fitting to fall gracefully over your curves on both sides of your tummy.

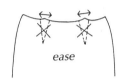

ease

Or change front skirt darts to **seams** to add a nice detail and to save on yardage in flat method construction. Draw a straight line through center of dart to the hemline. Cut pattern apart on the line and add seam allowances to both cut edges for conventional construction and only to the side front for flat construction..

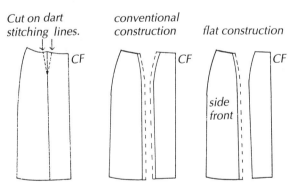

Cut on dart stitching lines.   *conventional construction*   *flat construction*

CF   CF   *side front*   CF

Narrow darts are easier to sew in Ultrasuede. Change one wide dart into two narrower ones in the back of skirts and pants for best results.

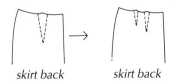

skirt back   *skirt back*

Extend vertical, double-pointed darts in jackets to the bottom edge. They will be easier to stitch and press **and** they won't pooch over your tummy. The longer dart is also more slenderizing. Add to the front side seam for adequate room through the hips in longer jacket styles if you extend the dart as shown.

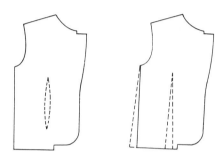

Darts–Conventional Method

We recommend this method because it's the easiest and it creates the strongest dart.

1. Fuse a 1" circle of lightweight fusible interfacing over the dart point unless interfacing already covers dart point, as in a jacket front. This helps prevent a pucker at the point.

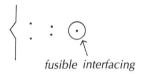

fusible interfacing

2. Stitch dart to a very fine point—it should just "melt" into the fabric at the point. Begin stitching at wide end of dart and shorten stitch length to 18 stitches per inch for the last inch or so. The last few stitches should be **at the very edge** of dart fold. "Chain off" a few stitches at point.

1/2"-1"

Lift presser foot and raise needle; pull dart toward you. Lower needle into edge of dart, drop feed dogs or dial down to 0 stitches per inch and stitch in place to anchor the chain without tieing a knot.

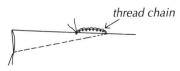

thread chain

3. Slash dart to within 1" of point. Press open over a ham with plenty of steam. Use tailor's clapper. Slip strips of paper under dart edges to prevent imprint on right side.

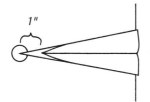

Darts – Flat Methods

If you are using flat method construction in the garment, you have the option of using either conventional or flat method darts. We usually do horizontal darts conventionally.

Lapped Dart–Flat Method

The lapped dart is our favorite flat construction method.

1. Slash vertical darts on the stitching line **closest** to center front or center back; slash horizontal darts on the upper stitching line, ending at the dart point.

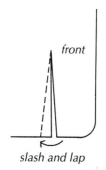

2. Lap the stitching lines and steam-baste with a strip of fusible web. Edgestitch, then topstitch 1/4" away from edgestitching.

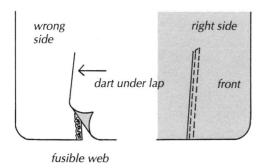

PRO TIP: To reinforce and fill in the point, cut an Ultrasuede triangle 1" wide at the base and 1/2" high. Fuse it next to the dart underlap edge at the point on the **inside** of the garment as shown. On the RIGHT SIDE, edgestitch and topstitch the dart.

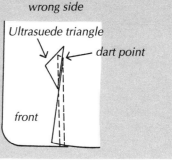

Slot Darts–Flat Method

The flat method "slot" dart is perfect for wide darts. It also has an interesting look.

1. Cut out dart wedge on the stitching lines. Cut a 1"-wide strip of matching Ultrasuede 1/2" longer than the dart.

2. Steam-baste strips of fusible web to the cut edges of the dart on the WRONG SIDE.

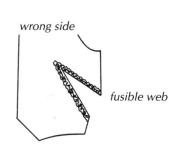

3. Center the Ultrasuede strip, RIGHT SIDE UP, under dart on WRONG SIDE of fabric. Working on a pressing ham, butt the cut edges together over the strip and steam-baste using a napped press cloth. Edgestitch.

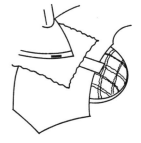

CHAPTER 12:
Zippers

It's easy to sew a zipper into an Ultrasuede garment using either conventional or flat sewing methods. We don't recommend a side zipper with either method. The side seam is usually curved and the zipper will not lay flat.

PRO TIP: For the easiest zipper application, use a zipper 2" longer than the actual opening. After sewing the zipper in, **unzip the zipper,** apply waistband or facing and cut away excess zipper above waistline edge. Today's synthetic zippers self-lock when the pull tab is pushed down so you can shorten them from the top.

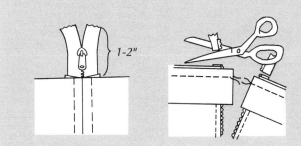

1-2"

Flat Method–Easy Centered Application

Pati developed this method in 1972 when she made her first Ultrasuede skirt.

1. Eliminate the center back (or center front) seam allowances by placing the center on the fold when cutting. **Carefully** slash on the fold.

slash on fold

QUICK TIP: Snip mark fold at top and bottom edges. Remove pattern piece and draw a line connecting snips on WRONG SIDE using a pencil and yardstick. Slash on line with long, sharp shears or use a rotary cutter and mat.

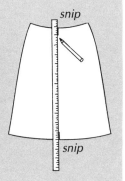

snip

snip

2. Steam-baste a 1/4"-wide strip of fusible web to WRONG SIDE of each center back edge. Place a 1"-wide strip of matching Ultrasuede fabric over the seam edges. Fuse in place with raw edges meeting in the center under the strip.

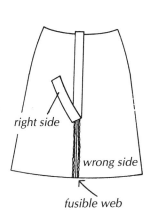

right side

wrong side

fusible web

3. Edgestitch. Carefully slit the strip the length of the zipper opening.

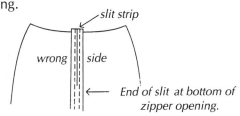

slit strip

wrong | side

End of slit at bottom of zipper opening.

4. Center 1/2"-wide Scotch® Brand Magic Transparent Tape® over the raw edges on the OUTSIDE to keep the slit closed while inserting zipper.

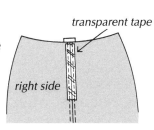

transparent tape

right side

5. Place basting tape on RIGHT SIDE of zipper along both outer edges. Peel away protective paper. Stick the zipper to the WRONG SIDE of garment, centering it over the slit.

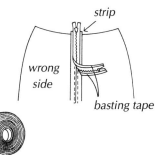

strip

wrong side

basting tape

6. Topstitch 1/4" away from the raw edges the entire length of skirt, catching the zipper in place. Remove basting tape. Remove transparent tape in direction of nap.

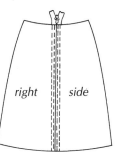

right   side

> **DESIGNER TIP:** For walking slit, slash from bottom and reinforce with a small piece of Ultrasuede on WRONG SIDE. Stitch on top of original stitching.

Flat Method–Lapped Zipper

(Illustrated for a center back opening)

1. On the right half of the zipper opening (underlap), make a 1/2"-deep snip at the bottom of the zipper opening. Turn under 1/2", tucking a narrow strip of fusible web between the layers. Fuse.

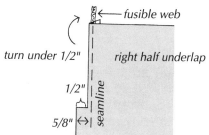

← fusible web

turn under 1/2"   right half underlap

1/2"
5/8" ↔ | seamline

2. Trim away the full 5/8" seam allowance the full length of the left half (overlap) of the garment. Fuse a 1"-wide strip of Ultrasuede the length of the zipper opening plus 1" to the underside of the overlap.

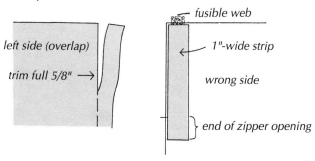

left side (overlap)

trim full 5/8" →

fusible web
1"-wide strip
wrong side
end of zipper opening

3. Edgestitch the length of zipper opening on the overlap. Pull the threads to the wrong side and knot.

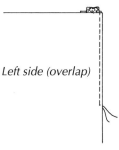

Left side (overlap)

4. Place basting tape on the face of the zipper along both outer edges. Peel protective paper from the right side only.

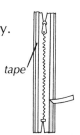

tape

5. Stick the zipper in place under the zipper opening on the underlap side of garment with fold next to zipper teeth. Edgestitch.

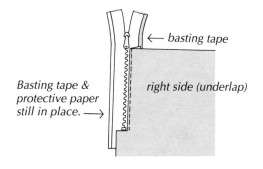

← basting tape

Basting tape & protective paper still in place. →   right side (underlap)

6. Peel the protective paper from the remaining basting tape. Lap left back over right and stick to zipper. Steam-baste the seam in place below the zipper.

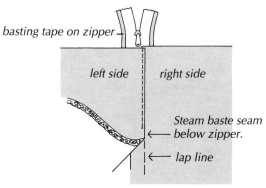

basting tape on zipper

left side   right side

Steam baste seam below zipper.

← lap line

7. Topstitch the full length of garment, 1/4" from the edge. Then edgestitch the remainder of the seam below zipper opening. Remove basting tape.

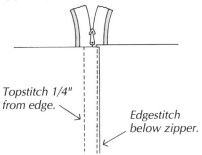

Topstitch 1/4" from edge.

Edgestitch below zipper.

Flat Method–Exposed Application

Use an exposed zipper application anywhere you want to create a decorative zipper opening for design interest. An exposed zipper is often the easiest choice for handbags. Use the same technique for separating zippers in casual jackets.

1. Cut a 3/8"- to 1/2"-wide opening for the zipper so zipper teeth and a little of the zipper tape are exposed. Use a sharp lead pencil and a ruler and draw the opening on the wrong side of the garment. Cut and steam-baste a 1"-wide facing to WRONG SIDE of opening.

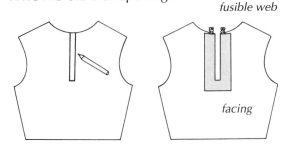

fusible web

facing

2. Fuse the garment to the zipper and edgestitch. Topstitch if desired.

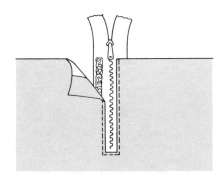

Flat Method–Separating Zipper

1. Trim away the seam allowances at **both** seam edges **plus** 1/8" to 1/4" on each edge, depending on the width of the zipper teeth. Do the same on the facings.

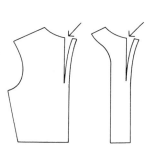

2. Fuse the garment to the zipper with the raw edges close to zipper teeth. Fuse the facings to WRONG SIDE of zipper. Edgestitch. Topstitch 1/4" from raw edges if desired.

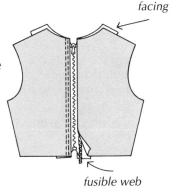

facing

fusible web

Conventional Method

Choose either a regular or invisible zipper and use your favorite sewing method. The following tips for a regular zipper may be helpful.

1. Choose a synthetic coil zipper for strength and compatibility with Ultrasuede fabrics.

2. For a smoother, flatter placket in lapped or fly front zippers, fuse overlap and underlap to garment.

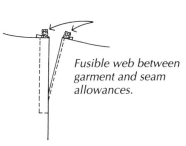

Fusible web between garment and seam allowances.

3. Use basting tape to hold zipper in place while stitching.

4. Use 1/2"-wide transparent tape as topstitching guide on overlap. Remove in direction of nap.

CHAPTER 13:
Waistline Finishes

We usually don't use a conventional waistband method on Ultrasuede pants and skirts because the flat method is so easy. If you prefer a completely conventional look, see the method shown for Ultraleather on page 115.

Waistband Application—Flat Method

Armoflexxx and Ban-Rol are monofilament nylon waistband interfacings available by the yard in several widths up to 2". We **love** them because they don't roll, stretch, wrinkle or crush or require preshrinking. Plus they're easy to use, lightweight and comfortable to wear. You couldn't ask for anything more in a waistband, could you?

1. Take a **comfortable** waistline measurement, allowing 1" for wearing ease. Cut a strip of Ultrasuede 3" **longer** than this measurement and **twice** the width of the interfacing you have chosen **plus 1/4"**.

2. Wrap the Ultrasuede strip around your waist and pinch together for a **comfortable** fit. Chalk mark where the band meets. This is either center front (CF) for a fly front opening or center back (CB) for a back opening.

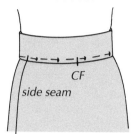

3. Mark the centers with chalk or erasable marker on the WRONG SIDE of the band.

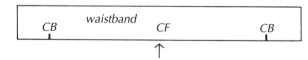

4. Fuse waistband interfacing to WRONG SIDE of waistband on the half that will be the **visible side** of the finished band. **Make sure nap will match garment nap.** Place the bottom edge of the interfacing 1/16" from the bottom edge of the waistband.

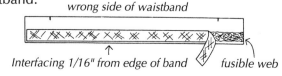

wrong side of waistband

Interfacing 1/16" from edge of band   *fusible web*

5. Lap the waistband to the waistline stitching line on the garment, matching centers. Pin with pins parallel to the cut edge. Try on garment and adjust waistband fit as needed.

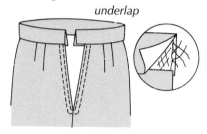

CF
side seam

6. Determine actual finished length of waistband allowing for a 1" underlap (or overlap if you prefer). Cut away excess band at each end. Lift and pull out several threads of the interfacing at the ends so the white interfacing doesn't show at the finished edges of the band.

underlap

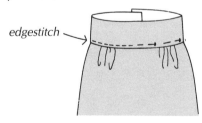

7. Edgestitch band to right side of garment, removing pins as you stitch.

edgestitch

8. Fold the remainder of the band to the inside over the interfacing. Steam-baste to the waistline seam allowance.

right side

9. Continue edgestitching around the ends and top of the band. Add optional topstitching 1/4" away from edgestitching if desired.

right side

Faced Waistlines

Smooth, faced waistlines come and go in fashion. If you're short-waisted, they are a perfect fashion detail for you because they create the illusion of better balance between your top and bottom half. In addition, you might be able to get facings out of scraps or unusually shaped pieces if you're short on yardage or don't want a conventional waistband.

Since we don't recommend front darts in skirts, first change the darts into seams (page 43). Then make your own facing pattern pieces.

Fold out and pin darts in skirt back. Lap and pin center front and side front skirt panels at seamlines. Measure 2" down from the top edge of skirt pattern pieces and draw a dotted line. Trace and cut new patterns from pattern tracing cloth or tissue.

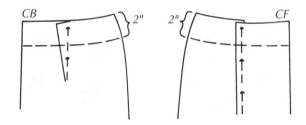

Faced Waistline — Flat Method

1. Trim away waistline seam allowances on facing pieces. Trim away the 5/8" side seam allowances on the **front facing only.** Cut from Ultrasuede.

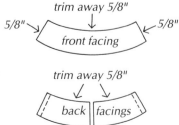

2. Using the facing pattern pieces, cut fusible weft-insertion interfacing with the stable crosswise grain going around the body. Trim away an additional 1/8" at the waistline edges of both front and back interfacings and at the side seam allowances on the front interfacing pieces. Fuse to the WRONG SIDE of the Ultrasuede waistline facing pieces.

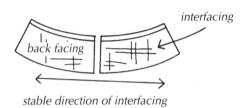

stable direction of interfacing

3. Assemble skirt and insert zipper.
4. Lap the front facings over the back facings at the side seams. Steam-baste and edgestitch.

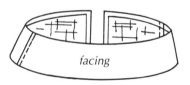

5. Fit the facing inside the skirt waistline, matching side seams. Trim center back edges of facing to clear the zipper teeth. Steam-baste skirt and facing together. Edgestitch (and topstitch if desired).

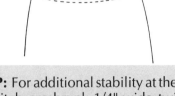

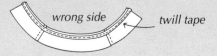

CHAPTER 14:
Collars

Flat method construction simplifies sewing any collar style in Ultrasuede because it eliminates the work of trimming, turning and pressing enclosed edges. Take special care when steam-basting layers together, since you will be pressing from the right side of the fabric when assembling the collar.

Collar With Band—Flat Method

1. Cut two collar and two band pieces. Trim the 5/8" seam allowance from **all** band edges and all but the neckline edge of collar pieces.

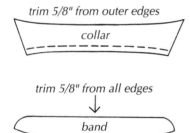

trim 5/8" from outer edges

collar

trim 5/8" from all edges

band

2. Cut fusible interfacing 1/8" smaller than the bands and the collar so it won't peek out at the raw edge.

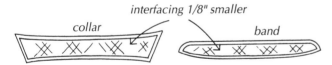

interfacing 1/8" smaller

collar   *band*

> **PRO TIP:** Interface **both** neckbands. It looks better. The neckband will be attractive worn buttoned or unbuttoned.

3. Apply interfacing to **upper collar** and **bands**. Mark the center fronts and center back on WRONG SIDE of band with marking pen.

CF   CB   CF

CB

interfacing

4. Staystitch the collar neckline and the garment neckline 1/2" from raw edge. Clip to staystitching.

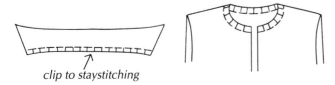

clip to staystitching

5. Lap band onto RIGHT SIDE of collar with raw edge just covering the staystitching. Center collar between center front marks you made earlier on wrong side of band. Pin with fine pins. (If you prefer, you can steam-baste the neckband to the collar.)

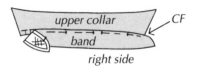

upper collar   *CF*
band

right side

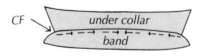

CF   *under collar*
band

6. Edgestitch directionally from center fronts to center back, removing pins as you sew. Pull threads to WRONG SIDE and tie securely.

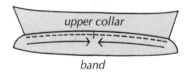

upper collar

band

7. Pin (or steam-baste) the neckband/undercollar to the neckline with pins parallel to raw edge. Edgestitch directionally from center fronts to center back. Pull threads to WRONG SIDE and tie securely.

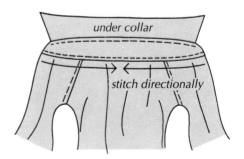

under collar

stitch directionally

8. Repeat with remaining neckband/upper collar, sandwiching the garment neckline between the two bands.

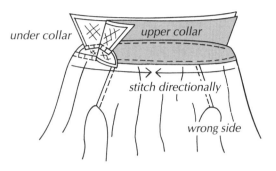

under collar
upper collar
stitch directionally
wrong side

9. Try on the garment, adjust the collar and pin collar layers together so they lay smoothly. **The raw edges may not necessarily match due to turn of cloth.** Place pins 1" from and parallel to the cut edge of collar.

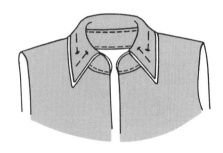

10. Slip strips of fusible web between the collars and neckbands. Steam-baste. Remove pins. Trim away any excess undercollar.

fusible web

trim excess

11. Edgestitch and topstitch as desired.

Collar Without Band—Flat Method

When attaching a collar without a band to a jacket or coat we prefer the look of a conventional seam where the collar is attached to the neckline. However, you can use a lapped seam if you prefer.

Convertible and stand collars usually end at the center front (CF). Styles with collar and lapels end at the "notch."

convertible collar

notched collar and lapel

stand collar

1. Trim seam allowances from the outer edges of upper and under collars. Leave 5/8" at the neck edge.

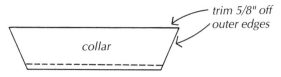

trim 5/8" off outer edges

collar

2. Trim fusible interfacing 1/8" smaller than collar and fuse to UPPER COLLAR.

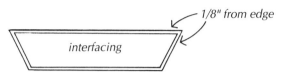

1/8" from edge

interfacing

3. Trim 5/8" seam allowance from front and neckline edges on both the garment and front facing. Leave seam allowance at the neck edge where collar will be attached.

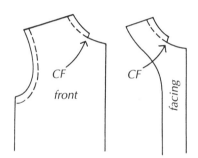

CF
front

CF
facing

4. Sew front and back facings together at shoulders. Press seams open and trim to 1/4". Staystitch facing and garment necklines. Clip neckline curves to make it easier to sew to straight collar.

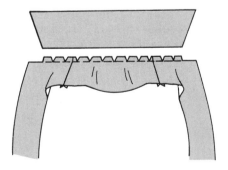

5. Stitch the **upper collar** to the **facing** neckline. Use a **conventional seam** and stitch directionally from center front to center back on both halves of the collar. Trim seam to 3/8". Press seam open.

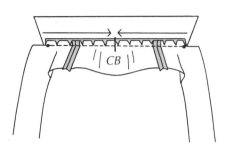

CB

6. Stitch the **under collar** to the **garment** neckline as described in Step 5. Trim seam to 1/4". Press seam open.

stitching direction

PRO TIP: Press the neckline seams open over the large curve of the June Tailor Board (page 25).

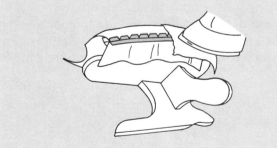

7. With WRONG SIDES TOGETHER, key (match) the neckline seams of the jacket and facing. Pin seamlines together, one on top of each other exactly, with pins pointing from center back to center fronts. Stitch together in the well of the seam. Sew on the upper collar side, stitching from center front to center back, overlapping the last few stitches.

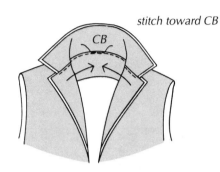
stitch toward CB

CB

8. Try on the garment and settle the collar into place. Pin the layers together as they lay, placing pins 1" in from and parallel to the raw edges of the collar and garment front edges.

9. Steam-baste the collar and front edges together with narrow strips of fusible web. Remove pins. Trim edges even with upper collar and garment front.

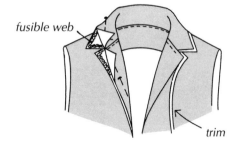
fusible web

trim

10. Edgestitch (and topstitch) collar and front edges. Pull thread tails to inside and tie off. See page 33.

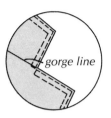
gorge line

Collars—Conventional Method

1. Cut fusible interfacing using the upper collar pattern piece. Trim seam allowances across collar points to remove bulk. Fuse to upper collar.

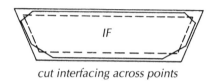
cut interfacing across points

IF

2. Assemble the collar following the pattern guidesheet. Trim the seams to 1/4", then press open on a point presser.

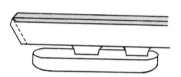

3. After trimming and pressing, **grade** the seams carefully, trimming the **upper** collar to 1/8" and the undercollar to 1/16". Turn and press using a napped press cloth, followed by a tailor's clapper to set the press. See pressing tips on page 24. Attach collar to garment following pattern guidesheet.

CHAPTER 15:
Hems

Marta says the only time you **must** hem Ultrasuede is when making a coat or jacket with a full lining attached at the bottom. Choose the most appropriate hem for your garment from these methods.

Flat Method Hems

- The **unfinished hem** is the easiest hem of all in Ultrasuede. It's a soft edge finish, especially nice for most skirts. Simply trim the garment to the desired length—if it wasn't precut to that length. Barbara uses the rotary cutter with a ruler and mat to make sure hem edges are perfectly and evenly cut. Edgestitch and topstitch if desired. In the softer suedes we prefer no stitching.

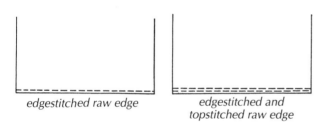

edgestitched raw edge   *edgestitched and topstitched raw edge*

- The **faced hem** is best for jackets and coats and essential when they are lined. Cut them the same width as original hem allowance. Faced hems are also appropriate on some skirts and on other shaped bottom edges. For shaped edges, use the pattern tissue as a guide and cut the facings **no wider than 3/4"**. Steam-baste to the WRONG SIDE of the hem edge. Edgestitch. Topstitch if desired.

wrong side

faced

PRO TIP: Since facings won't show on the outside, they can be pieced if necessary. Don't worry about the nap. To seam pieced facings together, overlap, steam-baste and edgestitch.

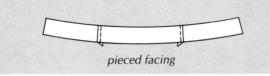

pieced facing

For design detail in both unfinished hem edges and faced hems, trim with scalloping or pinking shears, or add decorative machine stitching such as scalloping or decorative serging.

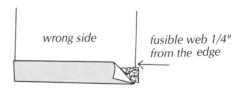

scalloped   *serged*

pinked   *scallop stitching and trimmed*

Conventional Method Hems

Choose this hem for a dressier look or when using conventional construction methods in the garment.

1. For **straight edges**, turn and press a 1/2"- to 1"-wide hem. Cut a strip of fusible web the hem width, minus 1/4". Position web with one edge at the hemline fold. Turn up hem and fuse using a press cloth. Do not press over the top edge of the hem to avoid an edge imprint on the right side.

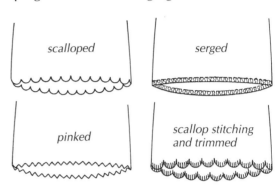

wrong side   *fusible web 1/4" from the edge*

2. For **shaped edges**, we really prefer a cut edge hem finish rather than a turned edge because it falls more gracefully. If you want a turned edge, trim hem to a width of **no more than 1/2".** Cut fusible web and fuse as described for straight hems.

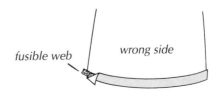

fusible web   *wrong side*

CHAPTER 16:
Sew a Simple Skirt

Straight, fitted skirts with a little softness around the waistline are flattering on most figures and easy to fit and sew in Ultrasuede. Avoid overly flared or circular shapes as they don't drape gracefully in Ultrasuede. Sew these shapes from one of the lighter weight Ultrasuede fabrics. See page 107.

If your pattern has front darts, we recommend eliminating them as they tend to "pooch" noticeably over tummies. Replace with soft gathers. See page 43. If there's too much front fullness, try taking in the front side seam allowance **only** when fitting the skirt.

Back darts are easier to fit and sew in Ultrasuede. Convert one wider back dart to two narrower ones for easier fitting, sewing and pressing. Or try soft gathers in back.

Sew an Ultrasuede Skirt from Less than One Yard???

Yes, but only if your full hip measurement is 41" or less. You will need a straight skirt pattern and a 45"-wide piece of Ultrasuede that measures the desired finished length plus 5". Use flat method construction and a centered zipper (page 45) at either center front or center back.

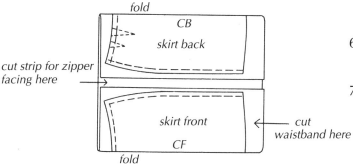

Basic Skirt Construction— Flat Method

Follow this easy skirt fitting and sewing order for any skirt style, referring to the chapters on darts, zippers, waistbands and hems as they apply to your pattern. After preparing your pattern for flat method construction (page 16):

1. Cut skirt to fit.

2. Insert the zipper in the center back or center front seam using a centered application. See page 45.

3. Pin in back darts. Easestitch front waistline or pin in soft pleats as desired. Lap the skirt front over the skirt back to the side seam stitching lines. Pin, placing pins parallel and next to the raw edge of the overlap on the right side of the garment.

4. Try on skirt and adjust to fit, moving and repinning darts, pleats and side seams to fit your curves.

5. Remove skirt, turn inside out and mark the location of the darts and raw edges of seams with a soft lead or chalk pencil. Remove all pins.

6. Permanently stitch and press darts. See page 43.

7. Steam-baste the seams, bringing the raw edges to the markings you made after fitting. From the RIGHT SIDE, edgestitch, then topstitch if desired.

easestitch

fusible web

8. Apply the waistband (page 48) and complete the hem as desired (page 55).

Conventional Method

Pati prefers this method as she can fine-tune the fit more easily with pin fitting (page 31). Follow the pattern guidesheet to construct your skirt.

CHAPTER 17:
Sewing Ultrasuede Pants

While we prefer the lighter weight Ultrasuede Facile for women's pants, culottes, soft trousers and jumpsuits, you might want to make men's pants from Ultrasuede. The more rugged look of Ultrasuede is especially appropriate for sporty or casual pant styles like jeans.

Before making pants, trousers or jeans in Ultrasuede for anyone, we strongly recommend making a trial pair in another firm fabric like denim to test and perfect the fit. Transfer any fitting changes you make to your pattern so you don't forget them when cutting your Ultrasuede pants. For help in getting a good fit, you'll find the most complete pants fitting information available in **"Pants for Any Body"** by Pati Palmer and Susan Pletsch. See page 127 for more information.

Conventional or Flat Construction?

The choice is yours and will depend on the look you wish to achieve. Flat construction seems most appropriate for jeans and other sporty designs. But, you may want to use conventional seaming in the inseam for ease of sewing. And the crotch seam is easier to sew and most comfortable when sewn conventionally.

Conventional seaming is more appropriate for dressier styles....and fitting is easier when the outseam is sewn conventionally.

Combination Lining/Underlining for Pants

We recommend a lining/underlining combination in Ultrasuede pants for added strength in a conventionally sewn crotch seam. Without support in this seam, Ultrasuede can tear away from the stitching line. (The first man we made Ultrasuede pants for can speak from a "bending" experience!) A lining also prevents the pants from sticking and climbing up the wearer's legs.

But, a lining doesn't add the same strength that underlining provides. We've solved the problem by combining the best of both techniques—individually **lining** each leg, then joining them at the crotch seam so that the crotch seam is reinforced with the extra

layer of lining fabric caught in the stitching line to take the stress of wearing. Trust us! This method really works!

1. Sew darts or tucks separately in each Ultrasuede pant piece and each corresponding lining piece. Press. Remember to convert front darts to soft easing or pleats to avoid darts that pooch over the tummy.

2. With RIGHT SIDES TOGETHER, stitch a back to a front pant leg at the inseam and the outseam using your choice of conventional or flat seaming methods. Repeat with the lining pieces. You should have four legs...two of Ultrasuede and two of lining.

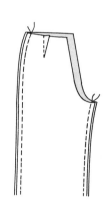

3. Turn the Ultrasuede legs RIGHT SIDE OUT. Turn the lining legs WRONG SIDE OUT and place each one inside the corresponding Ultrasuede leg, matching notches and raw edges. Pin.

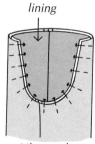

lining

Ultrasuede

4. Turn one set of Ultrasuede/lining legs INSIDE OUT and put the other set inside it with the suede sides RIGHT SIDES TOGETHER. Match and pin the crotch seams together. Stitch the crotch seam to the zipper opening.

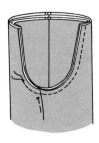

5. Complete pants, applying zipper and waistband, treating the two layers of fabric as one. When doing a fly front, do it conventionally. Hem lining separately from pant legs. Use your favorite hemming method for Ultrasuede from those shown on page 55.

> **DESIGNER TIP:** Copy ready-to-wear suede pants with interesting seaming details by cutting the pattern into shapes and adding seam allowances so you can "piece" them back together again. Start with a well-fitting basic pant pattern. Use **flat method** construction.

1. Fold out and pin darts. Draw in yoke line at tip of longest dart. Cut apart and add 5/8" seam allowance to lower leg only for flat method. Draw new "yoke" pattern piece; leave darts pinned out. You don't need them now.

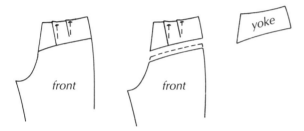

2. Add another design line in lower leg if desired.

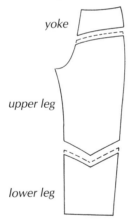

Convert a dart to a seam for an instant, permanent crease line—very slimming!

1. Fold pant pattern in half to establish crease line, lining up the inseam and outseam stitching lines from hem to knee level. Mark crease line from hem to waistline.

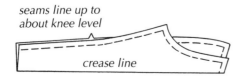

2. If dart isn't centered at crease line, draw a box around it, cut it out and move it into position.

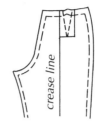 

3. Draw a line parallel to grain through center of dart in back and front leg. Cut apart on crease and dart stitching line.

4. Add 5/8" seam allowance to side leg panel. Use flat method construction, lapping and fusing the center panel over side leg panel. Work over curve of ham in upper curve where dart was removed when steam-basting.

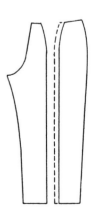

CHAPTER 18:
Sleeves

Don't let the thought of "setting in sleeves" in Ultrasuede make your soul quake! Usually sleeves are set in conventionally, but in some styles you may want to use the flat method.

Set-in Sleeves–Conventional Method

When Ultrasuede was first available, sleeve caps had lots of ease in them. Since Ultrasuede doesn't ease like wovens, it was often necessary to remove some of the ease. Today most sleeve caps have only 1" to 1 1/2" of ease which will fit smoothly into the armhole of an Ultrasuede garment with ample pinning.

If there is a little too much ease, use the "better-be-safe-than-sorry" method. Instead of removing sleeve cap ease before setting in the sleeve, machine baste sleeves in to see how they fit into the armhole. If there is too much ease, simply slip 1/8" (or more if necessary) of the sleeve cap into the armhole from notch to notch, then pin and check the fit again before stitching permanently.

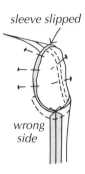

sleeve slipped

wrong side

> **CAUTION:** Don't remove sleeve cap ease unless absolutely necessary. Your aim is a smooth but softly rounded, pucker-free cap. It's really OK to scoot a little of the sleeve cap ease into the underarm area if necessary.

Use your favorite conventional sewing method to set in sleeves. Or try Marta's "pucker-free" set-in sleeve method for a smoothly set sleeve cap in tailored, **lined** jackets and coats. This method handles two steps in one. The bias strip is like a sleeve header that helps fill and shape the sleeve cap but you don't have to sew it in by hand after setting in the sleeve. It's already there!

Since it's not "pretty" we use this method only in lined garments. If your pattern doesn't include a lining, line only the sleeves. See page 101 for directions for cutting and attaching a sleeve lining in an unlined garment.

1. Cut a 1 1/2"x12" bias strip of Armo-Rite (HTC) or of a light to medium weight, loosely woven linen or linen-like suiting. Beginning at one of the notches, place strip on WRONG SIDE of sleeve cap with raw edges even. Stretch the bias strip to its fullest extent while stitching it to the sleeve cap. Use 6 stitches per inch and stitch just a hair inside the 5/8" stitching line. End at other notch. Cut away any extra bias strip at the end.

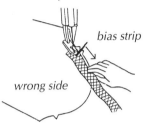

bias strip

wrong side

2. Voila! The sleeve cap is automatically eased and shaped and ready to pin and stitch into the armhole. You may find the sleeve still needs a little more easing to fit the armhole. A few extra pins will do the trick.

wrong side

3. Pin and machine baste sleeve into armhole. Try on for fit and adjust if needed. (See page 62). Stitch permanently and reinforce with stitching 1/8" from first stitching in underarm seam allowance from notch to notch. If necessary, use your fingers to smooth the ease after stitching.

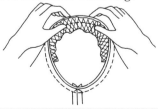

> **PRO TIP:** Marta suggests pinning the sleeves into the armhole with pins placed horizontally on the stitching line. That way you can **carefully** try on the garment without machine basting the sleeves and make changes easily before stitching permanently.

4. Trim the underarm seam allowance to 1/4" from notch to notch.

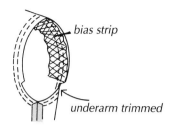

bias strip

underarm trimmed

5. Press the sleeve cap from the inside, allowing the tip of the iron to extend no more than 1/2" past the stitching line. Never press the cap from the outside.

Fine Tune the Sleeve Fit

1. Pin or machine-baste the sleeves into the garment.

2. Try the garment on. If it's a jacket or coat, be sure you're wearing the same weight clothing you plan to wear underneath. Slip shoulder pads in place if required. Lap and pin center fronts.

Check the sleeve fit.

Is the fullness in the wrong place? If you see puckers or pulls, clip the basting from the outside and tug the seam apart. Adjust the fullness so the puckers disappear. Some bodies need more front or back sleeve fullness. Since the pattern gives only an "average" placement for the fullness, it's OK to shift it so it accommodates your shoulder shape.

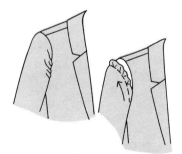

move fullness toward back   *move fullness toward front*

Set-in Sleeve—Flat Method

When your pattern has a flat rather than round sleeve cap as in dropped shoulder and shirt style sleeves, use flat method construction. Stitch the underarm of sleeve and garment conventionally in one step.

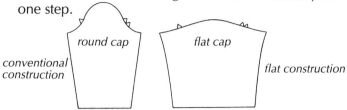

round cap   *flat cap*

conventional construction   *flat construction*

1. Complete the sleeve placket if there is one. See page 63.

2. Trim the seam allowance from the armhole edge on garment front and back. Mark notches and dots on the WRONG SIDE of front and back with chalk or lead pencil.

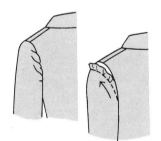

trim

wrong side   *wrong side*

front   *back*   *mark notches*

3. After stitching the shoulder seam in the garment, steam-baste a narrow strip of fusible web to the garment armhole edge on the WRONG SIDE.

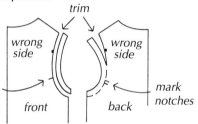

shoulder seam

wrong side

fusible web

4. Working over a pressing ham, place armhole edge at the stitching line on sleeve cap. Steam-baste in place, using a press cloth to protect the nap. Edgestitch, then topstitch if desired.

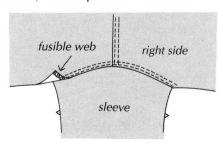

fusible web   *right side*

sleeve

5. Stitch the underarm seam RIGHT SIDES TOGETHER. Press seam open. Or use flat method construction if you prefer.

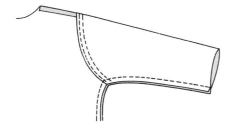

Sleeve Plackets

Eliminate tricky sleeve plackets on sleeves with cuffs. Before stitching the underarm seam in the sleeve:

1. Fuse a 1 1/2"X 2 1/2" piece of Ultrasuede, WRONG SIDES TOGETHER, centering it over placket area. Cut a rectangle of fusible web 1/4" smaller all around than the Ultrasuede so the edges of the patch don't show on the outside.

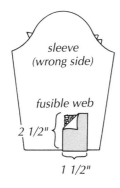

sleeve (wrong side)

fusible web

2 1/2"

1 1/2"

2. Make a 2"-long vertical slash through center of patch. Edgestitch.

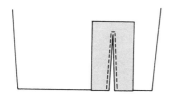

Cuffs—Flat Method

1. Trim away the seam allowances on all cuff edges.

2. For a one-piece cuff, trim the interfacing 1/8" smaller than the cuff at both short ends and one long edge. Fuse to the wrong side with one long edge at the foldline.

For a two-piece cuff, trim the interfacing 1/8" smaller than the cuff all the way around. Fuse interfacing to the cuff.

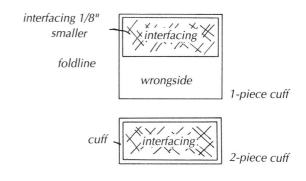

interfacing 1/8" smaller

interfacing

foldline

wrongside

1-piece cuff

cuff

interfacing

2-piece cuff

3. Pin upper cuff to RIGHT SIDE of sleeve with edge of cuff at seamline and pins parallel to cuff edge. Make sure nap direction on cuff matches nap on sleeve. Edgestitch. Trim sleeve seam allowance to 1/4".

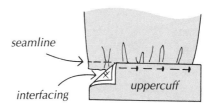

seamline

interfacing

uppercuff

4. Fuse undercuff in place on wrong side of sleeve, steam-basting the outer edges together. Complete the edgestitching and topstitching.

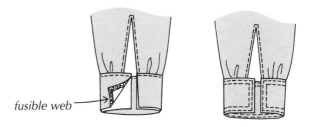

fusible web

Cuffs—Conventional Method

For conventional cuffs, follow the pattern directions.

Marta's Painless Placket

If you'd rather avoid the sleeve placket altogether, try this speedy "in-the-seam" placket that Marta discovered several years ago. It requires a pattern change before cutting and is best on a straight sleeve, but also works on fuller ones. Avoid it on sleeves with flat caps.

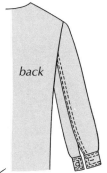

1. Draw a line through the center of the pattern placket markings parallel to the grainline.

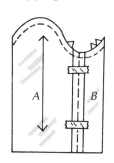

2. Cut along that line. Reposition "B" with the existing stitching lines overlapping.

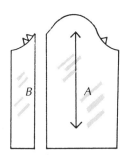

3. For **flat method** construction, add a seam allowance to "B" (the back half of the seam). For **conventional method,** add seam allowances to A and B.

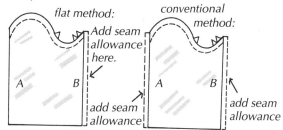

4. Cut sleeves. Mark the top of the placket opening with a snip on the back seam allowance and a pencil or chalk mark on the WRONG SIDE of the front seam edge.

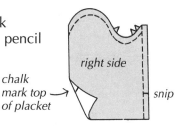

NOTE: If the sleeve isn't **completely** straight, overlap at the underarm seam intersection. Then line up the outside edges until they are parallel to the grainline. Otherwise your new sleeve seam would have one bias and one straight edge.

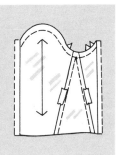

5. Edgestitch the cut edge of the placket opening. Topstitch if desired, stitching in a "U" at the top of the placket opening as shown.

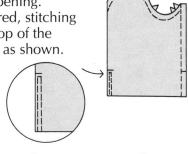

6. Follow the directions for a two-piece cuff on page 63; attach to sleeve while still flat.

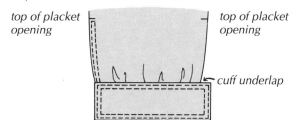

7. Lap cut edge of upper sleeve (A) to the seamline of the "under" sleeve (B) and steam-baste with fusible web, stopping at the top of placket opening. **Carefully** turn sleeve WRONG SIDE OUT to make it easier to stitch in the "tube." Begin edgestitching at underarm. Pivot and stitch on top of the stitching at the top of the placket opening and complete the topstitching.

PRO TIP: To use this placket with conventional sewing on Facile, Caress, and Ultraleather see **"Mother Pletsch's Painless Sewing".** (See page 127.)

64

CHAPTER 19:
Easy, Easier, Easiest Buttonholes

Buttonholes are easy and fast in Ultrasuede. We offer you three options—EASY, EASIER, EASIEST— and recommend that you make a sample of each method first so you can decide which one you like best for your garment.

In general, buttonholes at the front edges of garments are vertical when there is a band or vertical topstitching simulating a band look. Otherwise they are horizontal. Neckband buttonholes are always horizontal.

↑
CF

Horizontal buttonholes always begin 1/8" past the center front toward the front edge of the garment. Make vertical buttonholes on the center front line.

> **QUICK TIP:** Choose buttons and determine the length of buttonhole. Add button diameter to the thickness. Test buttonhole size in scrap and adjust as necessary.
>
> ↕ width plus
> length

Easy Windowpane Bound Buttonhole—Flat Method

It's easier to make bound buttonholes in Ultrasuede than in any other fabric, even if you've never made one before! Simply cut "window" openings in the Ultrasuede where you want buttonholes, then make the "lips" and topstitch them in place behind the window opening. It's that simple!

These directions are for buttonholes with a finished width of 1/4" but you can vary this size to suit your taste or to add design interest. You might even want to change the shape. Triangular buttonholes can be quite dramatic when done with lips in a contrasting color.

1. **Before fusing interfacing** to the garment, mark buttonhole locations on the WRONG SIDE of the fabric with a sharp pencil or chalk.

2. Make a template for the buttonhole window on lightweight cardboard. Draw a 1/4"-wide rectangle the desired length of the finished buttonhole and use a sharp scissors to cut it out of the cardboard.

> **QUICK TIP:** Make sure all buttonhole windows are marked and cut the same distance from center front. Position front end of rectangle on template the same distance as from the front edge of the garment to the front end of the buttonhole.
>
>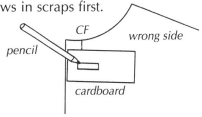
>
> CF ↓
>
> template

3. Center template over each buttonhole location and **carefully** draw around the rectangle with a sharp pencil. Cut out "window" with a sharp embroidery scissors. Practice cutting clean-edged windows in scraps first.

CF   wrong side
pencil
cardboard

4. Steam-baste interfacing in place on WRONG SIDE of garment. Cut windows in the interfacing. Be careful not to cut the Ultrasuede and trim away an extra 1/16" of the interfacing so it won't peek out at the edges of the buttonhole.

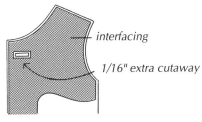

interfacing

1/16" extra cutaway

> **PRO TIP:** If interfacing is already fused to garment, try to gently lift edges around each window opening to trim it away. Or, **carefully** color the edge of the interfacing with a **permanent ink** marker that closely matches the Ultrasuede.

5. For **each** buttonhole, cut two strips of Ultrasuede 1 1/2" wide and 3/4" longer than the finished length of the buttonhole window. Machine baste lengthwise with RIGHT SIDES together, stitching 3/4" from the raw edges. Press lips open and fuse layers together with a narrow strip of fusible web. Trim lips to an oval and grade the layers to reduce bulk.

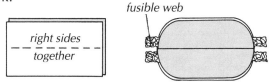

fusible web

right sides together

6. Center lips under each buttonhole window. Steam-baste in place with a "window" of fusible web. **After attaching facing** and finishing garment, edgestitch around the rectangle. Work from RIGHT SIDE and stitch through all layers. Remove basting between buttonhole lips and carefully slash facing through buttonhole opening using a sharp embroidery scissors.

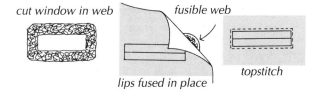

cut window in web   *fusible web*

lips fused in place   *topstitch*

> **DESIGNER TIP:** Conventional methods for bound buttonholes can also be used. Try your favorite method in a scrap or see **"Easy, Easier, Easiest Tailoring"** by Pati Palmer and Susan Pletsch.

Easier—Machine Buttonholes

Machine-made buttonholes look best and wear better when there is interfacing between the garment and the facing. Support buttonholes in single layer garments with a patch of knit or weft insertion interfacing on the wrong side. Cut and position the patch so the stable direction of the interfacing is in the same direction as the buttonholes so they won't stretch out of shape.

1. Make machine buttonholes through all thicknesses **after** facing is attached and garment is completed. You may need a longer stitch length. Stitches that are too close could "cut" the fabric.

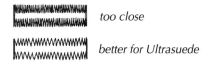

too close

better for Ultrasuede

> **PRO TIP:** Cord buttonholes to strengthen and prevent stretching. Stitch buttonhole over cording, gimp or heavyweight thread. Leave a loop at the end. When the buttonhole is completed, pull on cording ends until loop disappears. Bring the loose cord ends to the wrong side with a hand sewing needle, tie off and clip closely.

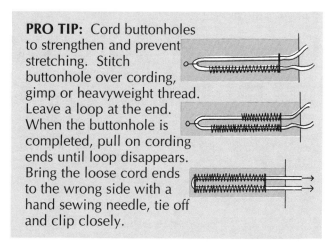

2. Slash completed buttonholes with a buttonhole cutter or **sharp**, double-pointed embroidery scissors. Place a pin at each end of buttonhole before cutting so you don't accidentally slice into the stitching.

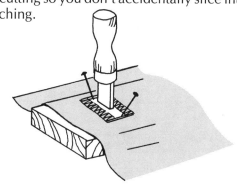

Easiest—Reinforced Slash

This buttonhole is often seen in Ultrasuede ready-to-wear. Designers use it—you can too!

1. After attaching facings, tuck a piece of fusible web between the garment and facing at the buttonhole locations and fuse the facing and garment together.

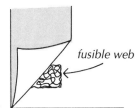

fusible web

2. Mark the buttonhole locations on the RIGHT SIDE with a piece of 1/8"-wide, double-faced basting tape cut the **exact** desired length of the buttonhole. Do not peel away the **protective paper**.

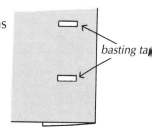

basting tape

3. Using 15-18 stitches per inch, stitch around the edges of the basting tape. Begin and end the stitching on one long side of the box, not at an end. Continue stitching around again over first stitching to reinforce. Remove the basting tape.

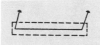

basting tape

QUICK TIP: If you accidentally stitch through the basting tape, clean the sticky residue from the needle with rubbing alcohol on a cotton ball.

4. Slash the buttonhole open with buttonhole cutter or sharp, double-pointed scissors. Place a pin at each end of the completed stitching so you don't accidentally slice past the stitching.

5. Use a tweezers to pull out any stray interfacing threads. If necessary, **carefully** color the interfacing edge with a permanent marking pen close to the color of the Ultrasuede.

Button Up in Style

Beautiful fabric deserves beautiful buttons. Your Ultrasuede garment is no exception. Spend some time searching for the perfect button and splurge if you must! Take a large scrap of your Ultrasuede with you when you shop. Make several slashes in the scrap so you can really see the effect of the buttons on the fabric.

You can also make beautiful covered buttons with Ultrasuede scraps and packaged button molds from the notions department. Try dampening the fabric to make it easier to cover buttons. Some stores and professional dressmakers offer custom-made covered buttons in several styles. Or you can send your scraps to Fashion Touches, P.O. Box 804, Bridgeport, CT 06601 and have them made. Their free catalog illustrates a variety of available button styles and prices.

Sew buttons on with two strands of regular polyester sewing thread. For tangle-fee stitching, strengthen the thread first and help it glide easily through Ultrasuede by running it through a cake of beeswax. Then place waxed thread between two pieces of paper and press with a warm iron to melt the beeswax into the thread.

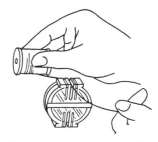

Be sure to allow enough thread for a 1/4"-long thread shank if your button doesn't already have one of its own. This prevents stretching and wear at buttonhole corners.

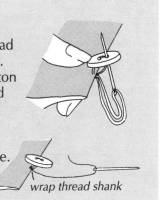

QUICK TIP: Try Pati's favorite way to sew on a button, adding a thread shank at the same time. Fold fabric back at button placement location and sew through fold. The farther away you hold the button, the longer the thread shank will be. Wrap the shank with thread and knot.

wrap thread shank

On coats and jackets, use a flat plastic backing button for added strength, stitching it in place at the same time you sew on your fashion button.

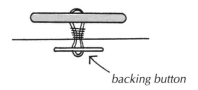

backing button

CHAPTER 20:
Pockets, Pockets, Pockets

Pockets are easy in Ultrasuede, whether they're of the patch, slot or welt variety. Conventional and flat methods are both appropriate.

Patch Pockets

Flat Method—"Lined" with Fusible Knit

1. Trim seam allowances from pocket pattern, leaving the hem allowance attached. Cut pockets from Ultrasuede.

2. Use trimmed pocket pattern to cut pocket interfacing from fusible knit. The knit will interface and line the pocket at the same time. Trim 1/16" from outer edges so interfacing won't peek out at pocket edge. Trim away hem allowance. Fuse to WRONG SIDE of pocket.

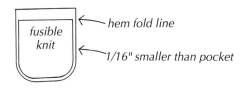

3. Trim 1/16" from side edges of hem allowance. Turn hem allowance to inside on fold line and press using press cloth and clapper. Edgestitch, then topstitch 1/4" away if desired.

4. Steam-baste, then edgestitch pocket to garment. Topstitch 1/4" away from first stitching if desired.

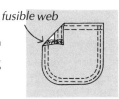

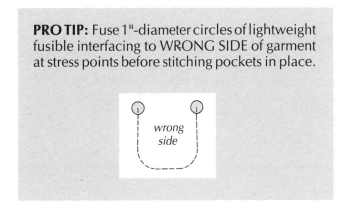

PRO TIP: Fuse 1"-diameter circles of lightweight fusible interfacing to WRONG SIDE of garment at stress points before stitching pockets in place.

Flat Method—Lined

1. Trim seam allowance from pocket pattern piece at side and bottom edges. Trim 3/4" from the side and bottom edges of pocket lining pattern piece. Cut pockets and lining. Stitch lining to pocket at top edge, RIGHT SIDES TOGETHER.

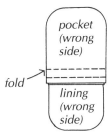

2. Press lining to inside at fold line. Use tailor's clapper to set the press at top edge. Steam-baste lining to WRONG SIDE of pocket. Make sure lining does not peek out past pocket edges.

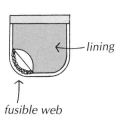

3. Edgestitch top of pocket. Topstitch 1/4" away if desired. Steam-baste pocket to garment. Edgestitch in place. Topstitch 1/4" away if desired.

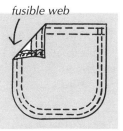

Patch Pockets—Conventional Method

Use a light- to medium weight fusible interfacing on the wrong side of the pocket. Complete and apply pockets following pattern guidesheet. Use a tailor's clapper to get sharply pressed edges. Steam-baste to garment so pockets don't slip out of place while topstitching.

Welt Pockets

Double and single welt pockets, with or without traditional menswear flaps, are beautiful designer details in Ultrasuede. Use either conventional or flat construction and our "goof-proof" methods for perfect pockets every time!

As with any designer detail, we recommend making a sample pocket first. When using the conventional method, careful pressing with lots of steam, a press cloth and the tailor's clapper will make the difference between beautiful pockets and those that scream "loving hands at home."

Welt pockets are often placed at an angle over the hipbone for a more slimming effect. They're also very tailored-looking as a back hip or side front pocket in skirts and pants and they're easy to add to any pattern.

Notice ends of welt are usually on "straight" grain and parallel to each other. The completed pocket looks like a giant bound buttonhole— easier than tiny buttonholes!

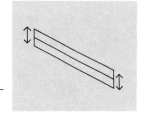

Slip a finished flap into a completed welt pocket and it becomes a more tailored mens-wear welt pocket. The outer edges of the pocket flap are also on straight grain.

When welt pockets are set at an angle, the pocket inside is at the same angle as your hand is when sliding it into the pocket.

Double Welt Pocket—Conventional "Windowpane" Method

We like this method for garments made with either conventional or flat construction methods as it's the easiest way to ensure perfect results with the **least amount of stitching** through this luxury fabric. Instructions are for a standard 1/2"x6" **finished** double welt pocket. Adjust dimensions for larger or smaller pockets once you've made this pocket and understand how it works.

First you create a faced "window" at the pocket locations.

Then you fuse the welts (windows) under window openings and edgestitch.

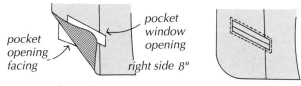

1. For each pocket, cut two 2"x8" rectangles of Ultrasuede. Two of these will form **one** double welt.

On reverse side of each piece, draw an **"UP"** arrow to show the **direction of the nap you used when you cut the garment.** This is very important if you want the welts to match the nap of the finished garment.

nap direction matching garment nap

2. For each **pocket bag,** cut an 8"x15" piece of lining. If pocket **will not** have a flap, cut a 3"x8" piece of Ultrasuede and stitch to one end of pocket bag as shown. (All drawings will show pocket **with flap.**)

3. On WRONG SIDE of garment, mark pocket placement lines ("box") with sharp lead pencil. Ends of 1/2"X6" "box" are on straight grain and parallel to each other.

4. For each pocket, cut a 3"x8" **pocket stay** from lightweight fusible interfacing. Draw two parallel lines spaced 1/2" apart on non-resin side of stay. Pink outer edges of stay, rounding corners.

} *lines 1/2" apart*

5. Fuse stay on WRONG SIDE of garment matching pocket placement lines. Draw ends of "box onto the stay. Machine baste around the "box" with a contrasting thread in bobbin.

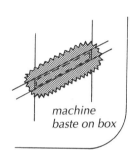
machine baste on box

6. Pin pocket bag over the stitched "box" on RIGHT SIDE of garment. Top edge of pocket bag should be 1" **above** top line of "box".

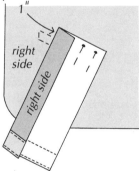
1"
right side
right side

7. On INSIDE, stitch around "box" using 15 stitches per inch. Begin and end stitching in the center of "box," **not** at a corner. Carefully remove machine basting.

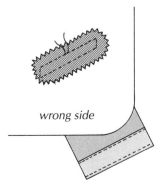
wrong side

8. Cut through center of "box" through both layers, stopping 3/4" from the ends. **Carefully** clip to corners.

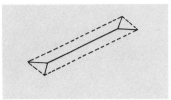

9. Turn pocket bag to inside. Anchor to a pressing ham and press on INSIDE. Use a tailor's clapper to set the press. Make sure pocket bag doesn't peek out on right side of garment.

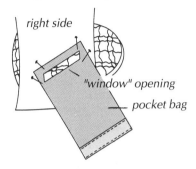
right side
"window" opening
pocket bag

10. RIGHT SIDES TOGETHER, machine baste through center of two welts, **with the arrows marking the "UP" direction reversed** as shown. Open out welts and press, using a press cloth to protect nap. Tuck a 1/2"-wide strip of fusible web between layers and fuse to add body and hold the press.

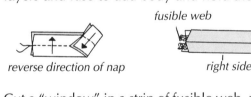
reverse direction of nap
fusible web
right side

11. Cut a "window" in a strip of fusible web, making the opening **slightly larger** than the pocket opening. Position web over pocket opening on WRONG SIDE and steam until just "tacky" enough to stick.

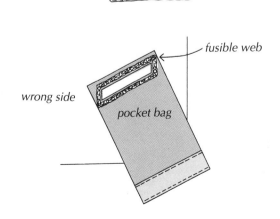
fusible web
wrong side
pocket bag

12. On RIGHT SIDE, center welt under "window" and steam-baste again, using a napped press cloth to protect the nap.

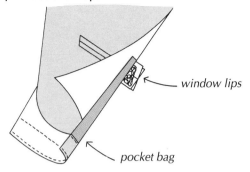

window lips

pocket bag

13. Edgestitch pocket opening to welts. Remove the basting between the two welts.

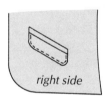

14. If pocket has a flap, construct it now using either flat or conventional method. Measure pocket opening and make sure flap will fit into it. Adjust flap size if necessary. See page 89 for flat method flaps.

15. Slip the completed flap into position through the pocket opening from OUTSIDE.

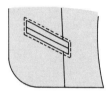

right side

16. On INSIDE, pin and stitch the pocket flap to the upper welt only.

flap

pocket bag

wrong side

17. On INSIDE, bring pocket bag up to cover welt with raw edges matching. Pin in place.

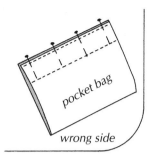

pocket bag

wrong side

18. On OUTSIDE, stitch on top of the previous stitching at top edge of pocket **only**, stitching through all layers. Pull threads to the inside and tie off securely.

19. Stitch the sides of pocket bag, rounding off bottom to prevent lint from collecting in corners.

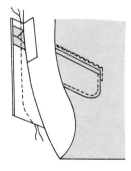

Double Welt Pocket—Flat "Windowpane" Method

Use this method if you prefer uniformity in construction and would rather have a raw edge finish around your double welt pockets. The method is a variation of the conventional windowpane method.

Instructions are for a standard 1/2"x6" FINISHED double welt pocket.

1. See the windowpane method for Steps 1-3 on page 86.

2. **Carefully** cut the "box" out of the garment using a small, sharp, double-pointed scissors.

right side

3. Unless you fused interfacing to entire front **before** completing steps 1 and 2 above, cut a 3"x8" **pocket stay** from lightweight fusible interfacing. Center and draw a 5/8"x 6 1/8" box on non-resin side of pocket stay. Cut box out of the stay and test over pocket cutout to make sure interfacing won't show at raw edges of completed pocket. Trim if necessary. Pink outer edges of stay, rounding corners. Fuse to WRONG SIDE of garment over pocket cutout.

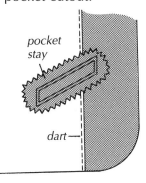

pocket stay

dart

4. Prepare the pocket welts and stitch them in place, following Steps 10 through 13 on page 88. If your pockets will have flaps, complete and apply them following Steps 14 and 15 on page 88.

5. On INSIDE, pin pocket flap to welt only. Stitch flap to upper welt.

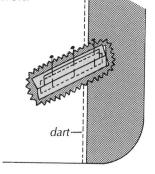

dart

6. Overlap and stitch pocket bag to lower welt with WRONG SIDE of lining against welt. Use a long zigzag stitch.

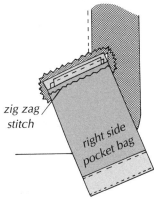

zig zag stitch

right side pocket bag

7. Complete the pocket following steps 17 through 19 on page 88.

Pocket Flaps

Pocket flaps are easy in Ultrasuede. Follow the pattern guidesheet for conventional construction.

Flaps—Flat Method

1. Trim away all seam allowances on flap pattern piece. Cut two flaps for each pocket from Ultrasuede. Trim away seam allowance plus 1/8" from all edges of interfacing. Fuse to WRONG SIDE of flap. Steam-baste flap to flap facing, WRONG SIDES together. Edgestitch the sides and bottom edges. Topstitch 1/4" away if desired.

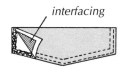

interfacing

NOTE: If flap is for a single or double welt pocket, trim only the seam allowances shown below. Prepare as shown, Step 1. Slip flap into completed welt pocket opening and stitch. See page 88.

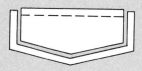

2. Steam-baste the top edge of flap in position on the garment. Edgestitch, then topstitch if desired.

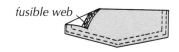

fusible web

Design Your Own Pocket Shapes

Consider reshaping pockets or flaps to add a little pizazz and individuality to your garment. Patch pockets and pocket flaps lend themselves to creative shaping in Ultrasuede. It's easy to stitch unique curves and corners when using the flat construction method because two layers of the same shape (pocket and facing or flap and flap facing) are simply steam-basted and then edgestitched together. Or, add a decorative band to the top edge of a patch pocket in a matching or contrasting color. The possibilities are endless when you give free rein to your imagination. "Borrow" ideas from magazines and mail-order catalogs, too.

Here are a few "shapely" ideas to consider. Experiment with these or your own ideas in scraps of pattern tracing cloth or other lightweight, nonwoven interfacing before cutting them from Ultrasuede.

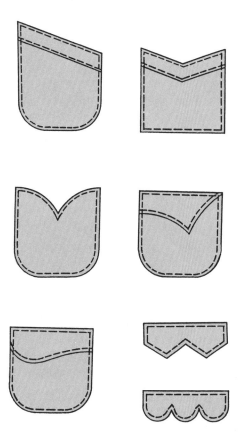

Super Easy Slot Pocket—Flat Method

What could be easier than edgestitching a slash? Marta developed this slot pocket, taking full advantage of Ultrasuede's best feature—raw edges that don't ravel. It's super-easy and best of all, it's super-fast, too. It's simple to add a slot pocket to any garment wherever you want one. It's also easy to tuck a pocket flap into a slot pocket.

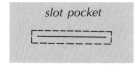
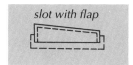

Directions are for a slot pocket with a finished length of 6". Finished size can vary as you desire. Upper pockets are usually 4" to 5" long.

1. **For each pocket,** cut the following: one 8"x15" pocket bag from lining fabric; one 2"x8" rectangle and one 2 1/2"x8" rectangle from Ultrasuede and from a lightweight fusible interfacing such as Whisper Weft. Fuse the interfacing to the WRONG SIDE of the corresponding Ultrasuede rectangles. Set aside the smaller rectangle for the pocket facing.

2. Stitch long edges of larger Ultrasuede rectangle to one end of pocket bag with the WRONG SIDE of the Ultrasuede next to RIGHT SIDE of pocket bag.

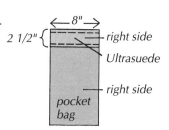

3. Using a ruler and a SHARP chalk marking pencil, draw 6"-long pocket placement line on RIGHT SIDE of garment in desired position. Poke straight pins through ends of placement line. On INSIDE, mark pins with soft lead pencil. Remove pins. Draw straight line between the two marks.

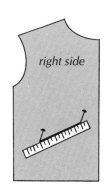

4. Center a 1/2"X6" strip of fusible web on WRONG SIDE over pocket placement line. Steam until tacky enough to stick to garment.

   Center pocket facing over fusible web with interfaced side against WRONG SIDE of garment and upper edge of facing 1" above pocket placement line. Fuse, using a napped press cloth to protect the nap on the facing.

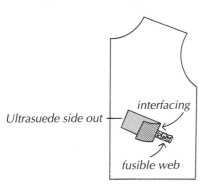

Ultrasuede side out — *interfacing*
fusible web

5. On OUTSIDE, center basting tape over chalked pocket placement line. **Do not remove protective paper.** Stitch around tape. Remove tape. Pull threads to inside and tie off. Topstitch 1/4" away if desired. Slash through all layers.

stitch around edges of basting tape

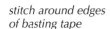

6. On INSIDE, stitch pocket bag to bottom edge of pocket facing 1/4" from raw edge with RIGHT SIDES TOGETHER. Press seam toward pocket bag.

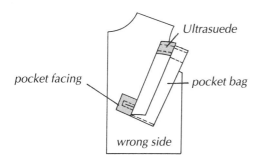

Ultrasuede
pocket facing — *pocket bag*
wrong side

7. Bring the bottom edge of the pocket bag up to match the top edge of the pocket facing and stitch together 1/4" from the raw edge.

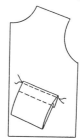

8. On OUTSIDE, tuck a 1/2"-wide strip of fusible web between the top edge of the pocket slash and the pocket bag. Fuse in place using a napped press cloth to protect the nap. Stitch on top of the previous edgestitching along the top ege of the pocket opening only.

9. On the INSIDE, stitch the sides of the pocket bag, rounding the bottom to prevent lint from collecting in the corners.

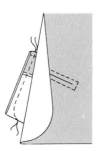

DESIGNER TIP: For a creative touch, consider shaping the slash and using a contrasting color suede rectangle on the pocket bag. Cutwork (page 120) would add yet another decorative detail.

CHAPTER 21:
Jackets and Coats—Flat Method Construction

A classic jacket or coat in Ultrasuede is a welcome addition to anyone's wardrobe. Seasonless, timeless and long-wearing, a tailored jacket or coat with collar and lapels is actually easier and faster to sew in Ultrasuede using flat method construction than sewing conventionally in traditional tailoring fabrics. If you've avoided sewing a coat because you think they're more difficult, think again. A coat is simply a "roomier, longer jacket."

For the speediest garment possible, we've consolidated sewing, pressing, and fitting steps into a more rational, timesaving order so you make fewer trips to the sewing machine and ironing board. Follow our quick and easy sewing order, disregarding details not in your pattern design. You'll be wearing your coat or jacket in no time!

If your garment has sleeve vents and/or a center back vent, refer to "Sewing Menswear," pages 103 to 104.

1. Prefit pattern, make necessary fitting adjustments (page 29-31) and prepare it for flat method construction following diagrams on page 17. Cut jacket or coat from Ultrasuede and transfer markings. See page 21. **Do not cut front interfacing until after garment has been pin fit.** Cut undercollar interfacing on the bias from weft-insertion or woven fusible interfacings.

2. Pin body of garment together, lapping seams as they will be stitched and placing pins parallel to cut edges. Try on and adjust fit, repinning darts and seams as needed. Make sure darts are in correct position for your bustline. You now have a garment altered to fit before you've sewn a stitch!

raw edge

3. Remove garment, turn WRONG SIDE OUT and mark the edges of all underlaps onto overlap using a chalk marking pencil or a soft lead pencil. Mark dart stitching lines. Remove all pins.

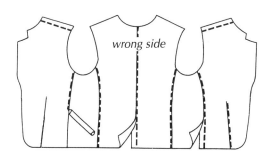

wrong side

4. If garment has a vertical front dart, cut front interfacing so it ends at the dart stitching line farthest from center front. Interfacing should extend past point into dart at least 1" for easier pressing. Pink inner edge of interfacing as shown. Do not fuse yet.

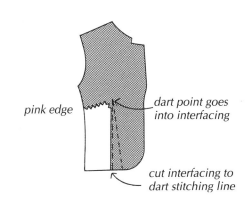

pink edge

dart point goes into interfacing

cut interfacing to dart stitching line

QUICK TIP: You may cut and fuse interfacing to the entire front piece if you prefer.

If there is no front dart, cut front interfacing using front pattern piece instead of the interfacing pattern piece.

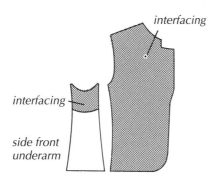

interfacing

interfacing

side front underarm

5. Trim 1/2" from neckline of the front interfacing. Trim away entire seam allowance plus an additional 1/8" along front, lapel, shoulder and underarm edges so interfacing won't show at the finished edges.

    Split interfacing at lapel roll line to make lapel lay flat. Fuse interfacing to the garment front and the lapel. Fuse underarm interfacing to side panel.

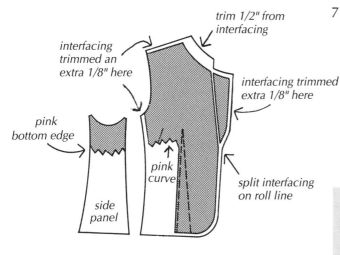

interfacing trimmed an extra 1/8" here

trim 1/2" from interfacing

interfacing trimmed extra 1/8" here

pink bottom edge

pink curve

split interfacing on roll line

side panel

PRO TIP: We usually don't tape the roll line in a woman's Ultrasuede jacket or coat unless sewing for a full-busted figure. In that case, use twill tape cut the length of the roll line, less 3/8" for a medium bust or less 1/2" for a very full bust. Pin in place with one edge along the roll line, easing in the extra fullness of the lapel. Fell stitch in place. This will improve the fit of the lapel over the curve of the bust and prevent roll line "gaposis."

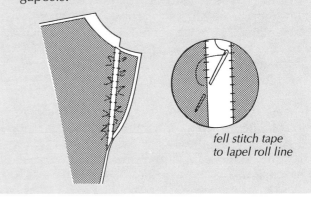

fell stitch tape to lapel roll line

6. Lap, steam-baste and stitch undercollar seam.

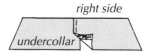

right side

undercollar

7. Trim undercollar interfacing 1/8" smaller than undercollar. Trim 1/2" from center back seam of interfacing. Fuse interfacing to undercollar, lapping it at center back. Place undercollar pattern piece back on top of undercollar and mark the roll line on the interfacing.

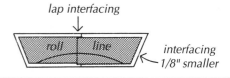

lap interfacing

roll line

interfacing 1/8" smaller

PRO TIP: For additional body in the stand of a tailored collar, fuse another layer of bias-cut interfacing just below the roll line.

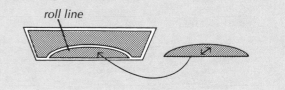

roll line

At the Sewing Machine

1. Stitch front darts (page 43).

2. Prepare patch pockets, (page 85).

At the Ironing Board

1. If darts were sewn conventionally, slash and press open.

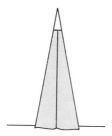

2. Anchor seam to a ham and lap the side front to the stitching line you marked on the WRONG SIDE after pin-fitting. Slip small pieces of fusible web in place at the raw edge of the **overlap** and steam-baste 1" at a time, smoothing any ease in with fingers.

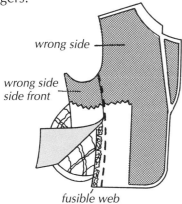

wrong side

wrong side side front

fusible web

NOTE: Use the same steam-basting method throughout the remainder of the garment construction. Steam-baste fusible web to the wrong side of each raw edge just prior to lapping and steam-basting it in place from the inside of the garment. That way there's no chance of the fusible web falling off and getting accidentally fused to the garment where it doesn't belong!!

At the Machine and Ironing Board

1. Edgestitch the side front seam. Topstitch if desired.

2. Apply patch pockets (page 85) or make welt pockets (page 86) in fronts.

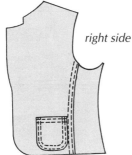

right side

At the Ironing Board

1. Trim away center back seam allowance on the **left back only.** See page 103 for back vent.

2. Working on WRONG SIDE, lap each of the following seams to the line you marked after pin-fitting. Steam-baste **lightly** for 2 to 3 seconds **only**. Lap the right back over left back to markings, anchoring with pins as needed. Lap the side back seams to markings on garment back.

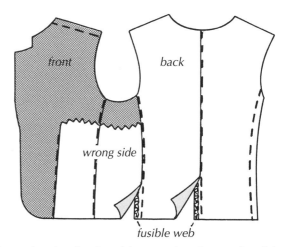

front

back

wrong side

fusible web

Lap the back shoulder to the front shoulder markings. Work over a ham and anchor with pins as needed. Trim shoulder seam allowance from front facing. Lap front over back facing at shoulders.

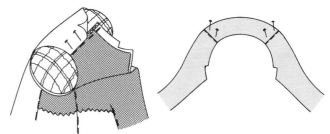

Lap the **under sleeve** over the upper sleeve. (See page 104 for sleeves with vents.)

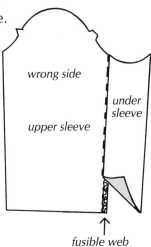

wrong side

upper sleeve

under sleeve

fusible web

3. Try on garment shell for a final fit **before** permanent stitching. If seams need adjusting, gently separate the steam-basted layers, scratch away the unmelted web, refit and steam-baste again with new strips of fusible web.

QUICK TIP: Remove stubborn bits of fusible web with rubbing alcohol.

At the Machine

1. Permanently edgestitch all steam-basted seams including the sleeve and facing seams. Topstitch 1/4" from edgestitching if desired.

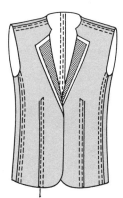

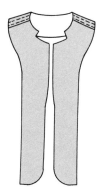

flat method darts

2. Staystitch garment and facing neckline seams.

jacket

facing

3. With RIGHT SIDES TOGETHER, stitch remaining sleeve seam in a **conventional seam.** Make a quick trip to the ironing board and press this seam open. You may also sew this seam using flat construction if you prefer—Marta always does it that way, but it is a skinny tube in which to work.

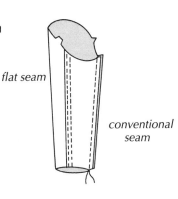

flat seam

conventional seam

4. Pin and machine baste sleeves into armholes for fitting. See page 61 for sleeve how-tos.

5. Stitch the **upper collar** to the facing neckline, clipping the **facing** neckline as necessary. Use a **conventional seam** and stitch directionally from center front to center back on both halves of collar, removing pins as you stitch. Trim seam to 3/8". Press seam open over padded long curve of June Tailor board.

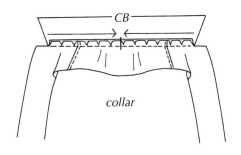

CB

collar

6. Stitch the **undercollar** to the **garment** neckline as described in Step 5, above, clipping the neckline as necessary. Trim seam to 1/4". Press seam open over padded curve of June Tailor board.

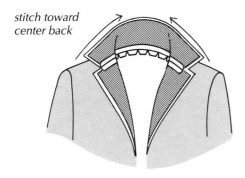

stitch toward center back

Check and Adjust Sleeve Fit

1. Try on garment with shoulder pads and check sleeve fit. Adjust sleeves as necessary and stitch permanently. See page 62.

2. Try garment on again. Tuck shoulder pads inside and adjust to your shoulder location. Regular pads should extend about 3/8" into sleeve seam. Extended or raglan pads should extend beyond and cup over the edge of your shoulder.

regular shoulder pad   *raglan shoulder pad*

3. Remove garment and loosely catchstitch shoulder pads in place along shoulder seam.

At the Machine

1. Assemble the lining and attach to the garment facings following the Quick Lining—Flat Method. See page 99, steps 1 through 6.

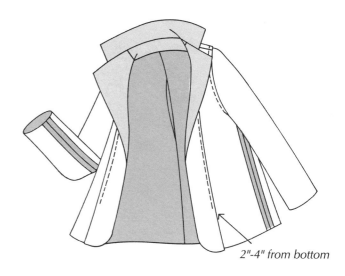

2"-4" from bottom

2. WRONG SIDES TOGETHER, match and pin neckline seams of garment and facing together with pins pointing from center back to center front. Stitch in well of seam from upper collar side, stitching from center front to center back, overlapping stitching the last few stitches. Remove pins as you sew.

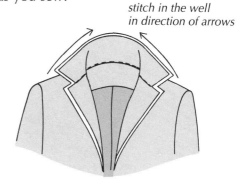

stitch in the well in direction of arrows

Time for the Final Fitting

Try on garment and smooth the collar and lapels into place. Edges are usually uneven because the upper collar and lapel were cut to roll under with conventional construction. Pin them together as they lay, placing the pins 1" in from and parallel to the raw edges around the lapel and collar as shown.

One last trip to the machine, a little handwork and—YEAH!!! Your jacket or coat is finished!!!

Edgestitch around entire outside edge of the garment, collar, lapels and bottom of sleeves. Topstitch 1/4" away from the edgestitching if desired. Pull threads to the inside and tie off.

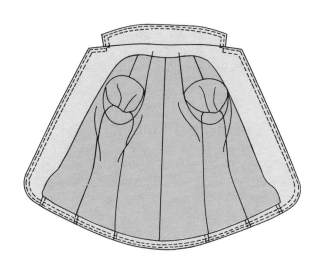

At the Ironing Board

Steam-baste collar, lapel and garment front and bottom edges together with narrow strips of fusible web. Remove pins. Trim collars and lapels evenly. Steam-baste sleeve facings to the bottom edges of sleeves.

To complete the lining hems see page 100, Steps 8 and 9.

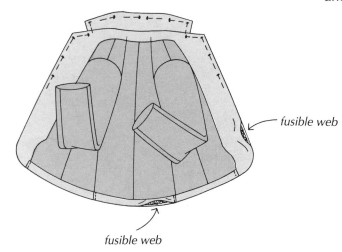

fusible web

fusible web

CHAPTER 22:
Lining Ultrasuede Jackets and Coats

Make your Ultrasuede jacket or coat easier to slip on and off and add wearing life with a full lining. See page 28 for tips on lining selection.

If your pattern doesn't include a lining pattern, it's easy to cut your own full lining pattern following our easy directions on page 102.

Quick-Lining—Flat Method

We think you'll love this super-fast jacket or coat lining for flat method construction. Assemble the lining and attach it to the facings. Then sew the facing/lining unit to the completed garment shell, do a little handsewing and your jacket or coat is finished and ready to wear! This method works on all jacket and coat styles and is illustrated here on a jacket.

1. Assemble the garment but do not apply front or hem facings. For garments with collars, stitch undercollar to body of garment and stitch upper collar to facing following directions for flat construction on pages 96 and 97.

2. Assemble lining and set in lining sleeves. When stitching underarm section, stitch a 3/8"-deep seam at the underarm, tapering back to the original seamline at front and back notches. This creates room for the underarm of lining to go up and over the sleeve underarm seam for a more comfortable fit.

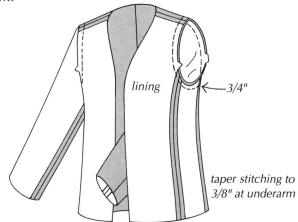

lining ← 3/4"

taper stitching to 3/8" at underarm

SERGER TIP: Serge lining together on your overlock machine and press seams toward the back.

3. With RIGHT SIDES TOGETHER, stitch lining to facing/upper collar unit, stopping 2" to 4" from lower edge. Stitch with lining side up. Press seam allowances toward lining using a napped press cloth.

2"-4" from bottom

4. From Ultrasuede scraps, cut facings for bottom edge of sleeves and jacket, making them the width and shape of original hem allowances. Nap direction is not critical. Lap, steam-baste and edgestitch facing sections together with a single row of stitching.

bottom facing   *sleeve facing*

5. With RIGHT SIDES TOGETHER, **stitch** jacket lining to hem facing. Stitch sleeve lining to sleeve facing. Turn seam allowances toward lining.

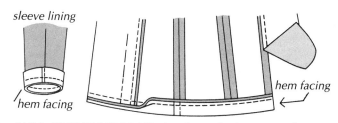

sleeve lining

hem facing

hem facing

6. With RIGHT SIDES UP, lap hem facing over the bottom edge of the front facing with lower edges even. Stitch in place.

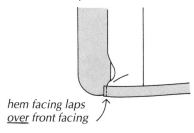

hem facing laps over front facing

99

FOR BLAZERS AND OTHER STYLES WITH COLLARS, STOP HERE AND REFER TO PAGE 98 FOR HOW TO DO THE FINAL FITTING AND STITCHING OF THE GARMENT.

FOR COLLARLESS STYLES:

7. Place facing/lining unit into jacket, WRONG SIDES TOGETHER. Tuck sleeve lining into sleeves. With all raw edges of facings and garment matching, slip narrow strips of fusible web between the layers close to the raw edge and steam-baste together. Use a napped press cloth to protect the nap.

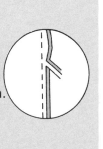

PRO TIP: It's almost impossible to cut facing edges to match garment edges exactly, so don't even try. Cut as carefully as possible. After fusing outside edges together, trim to straighten. You'll need a **very steady hand** and **very sharp scissors.** Or use rotary cutter, mat and ruler.

Edgestitch along outer edges of jacket and bottom edges of sleeves. Stitch from RIGHT SIDE, beginning and ending at side back or underarm seam. Topstitch 1/4" away from edgestitching if desired. Where stitching meets, backstitch carefully or pull threads to the wrong side and tie off.

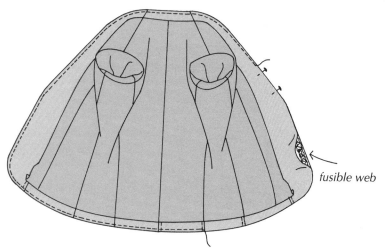

fusible web

WOW!! Don't you love it? No hand hemming! A "jump hem" forms at the bottom edge of the jacket and sleeves so lining moves with you comfortably without making unsightly "pulls" on the outside.

8. Smooth the extra fullness of lining down at the front facing edges. Slipstitch in place.

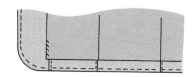

9. Hand tack sleeve lining to jacket sleeve seam allowances at shoulder, underarm and front armhole to prevent facing from pulling to outside at front edge. This is especially necessary with notched collar garments.

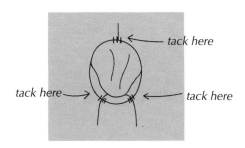

tack here
tack here
tack here

Quick Lining—Conventional Method

For conventionally sewn jackets and coats use the quick lining method as shown above with the following minor changes.

1. Complete Steps 1 through 3, page 99. Do not hem the jacket or the sleeves yet.

2. Pin facing/lining unit to jacket, RIGHT SIDES TOGETHER. Stitch, trim and grade seam. See **"Easy, Easier, Easiest Tailoring"** by Pati Palmer and Susan Pletsch for additional helpful information on stitching perfect collars and lapels. Press seam open over padded June Tailor Board.

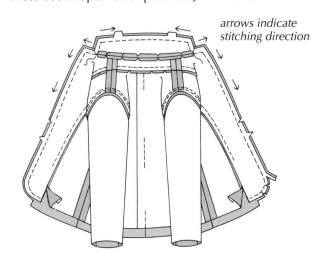

arrows indicate stitching direction

3. Turn garment right side out. Press outside edges using lots of steam, a napped press cloth and tailor's clapper. It is usually necessary to press two to three times in an area to get a clean, sharp press on conventional seams.

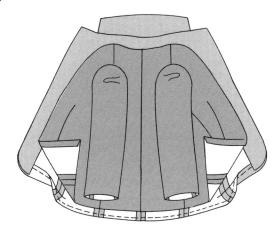

4. Machine stitch 5/8" from front facing and 1/4" from the bottom edge of jacket and sleeves. It is easier to hem lining to garment by catching hand stitches to this row of stitching rather than trying to stitch through Ultrasuede.

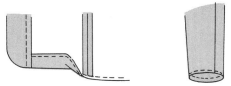

5. To hem jacket and sleeves, turn and press up hem allowances. For shaped bottom edges, ease out excess fullness with machine basting. Cut fusible web the width of hem **less 1/4"**. Position web with one edge at hem fold. Fuse being careful not to press over the top edge of hem.

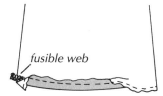

fusible web

ease fullness in shaped hems with machine basting

6. Press under 1/4" at lower edge of lining and at lower edge of sleeve linings. Pin lining to jacket and sleeve hems, matching raw edge of lining to raw edge of hem. Slipstitch folded edge of lining to machine stitching.

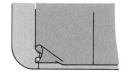

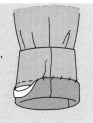

QUICK TIP: Turn bottom edge of sleeve back on itself when pinning and hemming the lining. It's easier to handle this way since the sleeve is such a small cylinder.

6. Smooth extra lining down at front facing edges and slipstitch to facing.

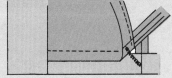

NOTE: If you prefer, hem a coat lining separately from the coat by hand or machine. It should be 3/4" shorter than the finished length of the coat. Machine stitch the raw edge at the bottom of the lining to the front facings to finish. Use swing tacks to hold the lining in place at the side seams.

Partial Linings are Also an Option

If you live in a warm, humid climate, you may be more comfortable in an unlined Ultrasuede jacket or coat. Or you might simply prefer the weightlessness of an unlined garment. If so, we recommend lining the sleeves to make it easier to slip them on over other garments. Some patterns include a pattern pieces for a partial lining. Here's how to line the sleeve in a jacket or coat when your pattern doesn't include it.

1. Use garment sleeve pattern piece to cut sleeve lining, cutting away the sleeve hem allowance.

2. Assemble the sleeve lining following the guidesheet instructions for the sleeve. Press seams open or to one side.

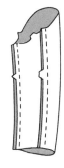

3. Machine baste 5/8" and 3/8" from raw edge between notches over sleeve cap. Staystitch underarm between notches 3/8" from raw edge.

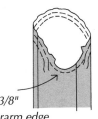

staystitch 3/8" from underarm edge

4. Slip sleeve lining over sleeve, WRONG SIDES TOGETHER, placing pins only at notches and other construction markings.

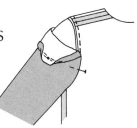

5. Pull on bobbin threads to ease lining until sleeve cap fits armhole. Don't pull too tightly. Turn under sleeve lining, clipping underarm curve to staystitching as necessary. Pin lining to sleeve and slipstitch in place.

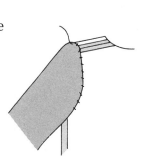

How to Cut a Full Lining Pattern for a Jacket or Coat

1. Place front facing pattern piece on jacket front pattern piece and mark facing edge with dotted line. Measure and mark 1 1/4" past dotted line **toward front edge** of jacket. This is the cutting line for the lining.

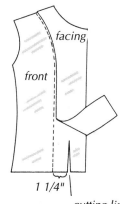

facing

front

1 1/4"

cutting line for lining

2. Place back neck facing pattern piece on jacket back pattern piece and repeat above procedure.

cutting line

1 1/4"

back neck facing

3. Turn up and pin hem allowance at bottom edge of jacket front, back, underarm panels and sleeves. If sleeve has a vent, eliminate it by folding it under.

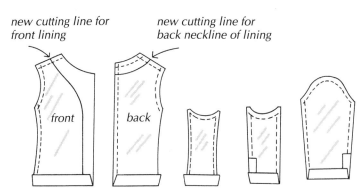

new cutting line for front lining

new cutting line for back neckline of lining

front

back

4. Trace lining pattern pieces you've created onto pattern tracing cloth or tissue paper, **adding 1" along entire center back for a wearing pleat.** Mark pleat stitching locations as shown.

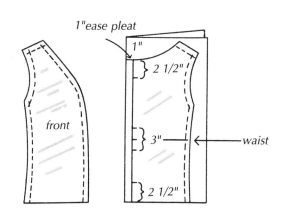

1"ease pleat

1"

2 1/2"

front

3" — *waist*

2 1/2"

CHAPTER 23:
Sewing Menswear

Ultrasuede is a natural for menswear—masculine, rugged looking, yet lightweight and functional. Since it tailors so well, it's great for men's jackets, coats and sportcoats. One of the spiffiest men's raincoats we've seen yet was a taupe Facile trenchcoat—absolutely gorgeous and oh-so-practical!

If you would rather start with a smaller investment with fewer fitting and sewing challenges, make a man's Ultrasuede vest. The back of a man's vest is most often done in a lining fabric. That leaves only the front section in Ultrasuede—a quick and inexpensive, yet impressive and sure-to-be-appreciated gift!

Casual jackets are terrific in Facile and very pricey in ready-to-wear ($295 in one catalog!). Or, how about Ultraleather for a man's bomber jacket? Even Caress can get into the act as a soft and sensuous man's shirt. Marta suggests making a man's shirt in Caress or Facile if you want to surprise him, since you can easily compare a shirt pattern to one of his own for a good fit without actually fitting it on him. In other words, don't try to surprise him with an Ultrasuede sportcoat—you need to fit it to him.

Sewing Tailored Ultrasuede Menswear

Men's Ultrasuede jackets and coats are usually more structured than women's wear; the shape is more defined.

Most men's jacket patterns suggest interfacing the entire jacket front, then adding a second piece of shaping—the "chest piece." That's easy with fusible interfacings.

chest piece

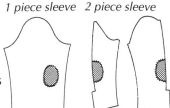

1 piece sleeve   2 piece sleeve

We also recommend stabilizing the elbows with an oval of fusible knit interfacing for longer wear. Do this in women's jackets, too, if you wish.

Although we don't feel taping the roll line is essential in a woman's Ultrasuede jacket, we recommend it for a man's jacket because of the longer roll line. Here's how.

Place one edge of preshrunk, 1/4"-wide twill tape along the roll line with the other edge lapping onto the chest piece. Hand sew both edges in place with felling stitches.

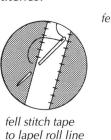

fell stitching

fell stitch tape to lapel roll line

FIT TIP: To prevent roll line "gaposis", cut the twill tape 1/2" shorter than the roll line and pin to roll line, distributing fullness so most of it falls in the middle third of the roll line area. Fell stitch in place as shown above.

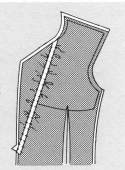

Vents—Flat Construction

Back vents and vented two-piece sleeves require the following special handling in **flat method construction**.

Center Back Seam with Vent—Flat Method Construction

1. Cut away the vent and the center back seam allowance on the **left** back. Save the vent piece to use as the facing.

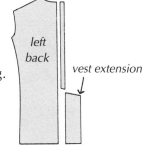

left back

vest extension

2. On INSIDE, steam-baste vent facing in place at cut edge. Edgestitch. Topstitch 1/4" away. Pull threads through to inside and tie off.

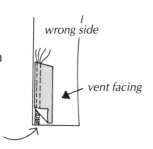

wrong side

vent facing

fusible web

3. Lap LEFT back over right back to the seamline and steam-baste, stopping 5/8" below top edge of vent extension. Work over a ham or seam roll **with a napped press cloth.** Edgestitch and topstitch, ending where you ended steam-basting.

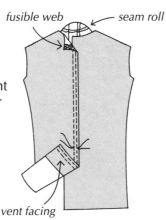

fusible web   *seam roll*

vent facing

4. On inside, fold RIGHT back extension under 5/8" and steam-baste with a narrow strip of fusible web. Edgestitch and topstitch. Pull threads to inside and tie off. Tack right vent to left at upper edge.

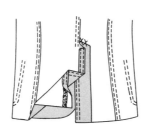

5. Complete jacket as shown on pages 93 to 98, preparing the lining with vent following pattern guidesheet. When stitching the jacket back hem facings to lining, stop 2" from vent opening edges.

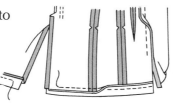

6. Pin lining to jacket above vent and along vent extensions. Slipstitch bottom edge of lining to facing. Sew lining to vents, smoothing lining to create "jump hem."

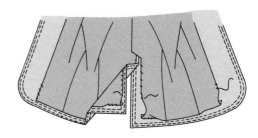

Two-piece Sleeve with Vent— Flat Method Construction

1. Stitch the underarm seam using conventional or flat seaming. For flat method, upper sleeve overlaps the under sleeve. Steam-baste outer edges of sleeve facing to sleeve, WRONG SIDES together. Edgestitch and topstitch, ending at top edge of facing. Pull threads to inside and tie.

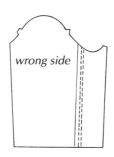   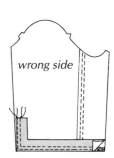

wrong side   *wrong side*

2. Working over a seam roll, steam-baste upper sleeve over remaining under sleeve seam allowance, ending at upper edge of facing. Edgestitch and topstitch sleeve seam, connecting with previous stitching. Pull threads to inside and tie off securely.

right side

3. After completing jacket, slipstitch sleeve lining to sleeve facing as shown in pattern guidesheet.

CHAPTER 24:
Caring for Ultrasuede Garments

YES!!! You can machine wash and dry your finished Ultrasuede, Facile and Caress garments IF you've followed our guidelines for preshrinking and applying interfacings and other shaping fabrics and notions. Ready-to-wear garments made of these fabrics sometimes require dry cleaning because manufacturers don't make it a practice to preshrink the components. Rayon or acetate linings are often used in ready-to-wear and must be dry cleaned only. You may wish to dry clean traditionally tailored coats and jackets. If so, we recommend asking for "dry-clean only" so you can do any touch-up pressing needed yourself. See Step 6, below.

With a little TLC, your luxurious Ultrasuede garments will look like new a long, long time. To launder Ultrasuede fabrics, follow these guidelines for best results.

1. Be gentle. Use warm water in the washer to relax the fabric but a cool rinse to avoid setting wrinkles during the spin cycle. You'll get the best results with gentle agitation and a permanent press cycle. Wash with other garments of similar colors in a normal-sized load.

2. Pretreat stains. Dow Spray 'n Wash® is particularly effective on grease and food. Water-soluble hair spray usually removes ballpoint ink. Rinse out the "ring" it may leave with water. Some minor cigarette burns can be gently scraped and brushed with a toothbrush to restore the nap. Serious burns may have to be cut out and patched. Sometimes they become a challenge to your creativity. Depending on the location of the "culprit" you may be able to hide or disguise them with appliques, beading or fabric painting or a number of other creative techniques featured in this book.

3. Use a mild detergent. When washing white and pastel garments, **avoid blue-colored detergents,** whether liquid or powdered. The blue dyes are fugitive and will permanently alter the color of your light-colored Ultrasuede garments.

4. Tumble dry at a moderate temperature setting **for 20 minutes only** to fluff the fibers and remove excess water. Check the load after twenty minutes. If the garment is still wet, continue drying until slightly damp. Overdrying damages polyester

fibers, causing them to wear out and pill. It also causes thread shrinkage. We've seen disasters— terribly puckered seams because the polyester thread tightened up due to overheating and overdrying.

5. Hang to finish drying. If the seams look at all puckered when you hang the garment to dry, lightly tug on every seam until the puckers are gone and the garment will dry smoothly.

6. If necessary, do touch-up pressing at a "low synthetic" setting with a gentle pressing motion. Press from the wrong side whenever possible. **Always use a wool or other napped surface press cloth when pressing from the right side.** Keep top pressing to a minimum!

7. Store your Ultrasuede garments as you would any other fine garment on a padded or wooden hanger. Fold pants and skirts over a padded hanger bar to avoid clamp marks. Or fold a scrap of Ultrasuede or wool flannel over the waistband to pad it and protect it from clamp marks.

Ultrasuede Recycled!

Ultrasuede garments are practically indestructible but fashion does change and sometimes stains are impossible to remove or a cigarette burn can't be disguised with creative measures or the elbows do wear out of your favorite jacket. Then it's time to consider restyling.

For example, make a too-short coat into a skirt, then use the remaining scraps to trim a wool jacket for a "new" coordinating outfit. Restyle a jacket into a vest when sleeves are too worn to salvage. Save all scraps for applique and accessory projects or cut an outdated or damaged garment into narrow strips and try your hand at weaving with Ultrasuede or knitting with Ultrasuede Facile. See color section.

If you have small children, Marta recommends using a double layer of Ultrasuede for patching their jeans and other playclothes. Her rough and tumble son wore through the denim long before the patches wore out! You can even turn the patches into creative appliques while you're at it. Recycling Ultrasuede is fun and easy!

CHAPTER 25:
Facile and Caress—The "Softies"

Made by a patented process, lightweight Facile and its feather-light cousin Caress are nonwoven fabrics of 60% polyester fibers and 40% non-fibrous polyurethane, just like the original but heavier Ultrasuede. The microfibers used to make them are invisible to the naked eye. Just think—one gram of Caress fiber is so fine it would stretch to the moon!

Like Ultrasuede, these two lighter versions have the fashion appeal of suede without any of the disadvantages—they won't crock, nick, pill, fray, water-spot or stiffen. They retain their shape during wear and they don't bag or stretch out of shape.

The packability of Ultrasuede has always been part of its appeal; it sheds wrinkles as soon as it's out of the suitcase. However, Facile, and especially Caress, the lightest in weight, will wrinkle, particularly in areas of high humidity.

The real appeal of Facile and Caress is their drapability! While Ultrasuede can be only slightly gathered or pleated, Facile and Caress can be **lavishly** tucked, pleated, gathered and shirred. In short, they can be sewn into the same designs as any other soft fabric, using **conventional** sewing methods. Facile is somewhat heavier than Caress but both are considered soft, drapable fabrics. In some cases, it may be difficult to distinguish between Facile and Caress because different dyes weigh more than others. Check the label.

Pattern Selection

Let your imagination soar! Almost anything can be made from these two sumptuous fabrics. While Ultrasuede is best suited to more tailored, structured styles, patterns for Facile and Caress should be chosen to show off their soft drapability. Consider blouses with deep dolman sleeves, supple jumpsuits, richly draped and wrapped dresses, very full culottes, loose, flowing jackets and capes. Caress is **so** soft, supple and lightweight, you can choose very full styles without the worry of adding too much bulk to your figure. Try a skirt with unpressed knife pleats or lots of gathers, for example. These two fabrics are knockouts in dressier evening wear designs, too. Barbara's Caress camisole and soft skirt ensemble (page 73) is evidence of that.

International fashion designers have used these luscious lightweights in innovative designs. Koos van den Akker creates dashing sportswear in Facile, combining it with his signature patchwork and applique. Caress lends itself to the romantic look of smocking, as seen in Molly Parnis creations. Other designers have done color-blocking with Facile and Caress and some have quilted them for even more textural interest. Scraps of either make truly wonderful and exciting appliques on everything from sweater knits to chambray shirts.

How Much Yardage to Buy?

Facile and Caress are spendy by any standard. Both are even more difficult and costly to manufacture than Ultrasuede, so the price for each is about the same at over $50 a yard for 45"-wide fabric. Remember, this is an initial expense only—they can be machine washed and dried so you won't have spendy suede dry cleaning bills.

Still, you'll want to plan carefully so you purchase only the exact yardage you need for your pattern. Planning ahead can save from $5 to $50. Watch for sales, too. Some fabric stores regularly offer their Ultrasuede fabrics at 20% to 30% off, knowing it will be just the incentive many high-fashion sewers need to become **hooked** on these luxurious fabrics. If you're unable to find them in your local stores, consider the many fine mail-order sources which advertise in sewing publications such as **SEW NEWS** magazine.

Like all suedes, Facile and Caress have a napped surface. Check the yardage chart on the pattern envelope for 45"-wide fabric "**With Nap**." But before you buy, let's look at some ways to save on yardage with these two fabrics.

1. Patterns with lots of smaller pieces require less fabric than "easy" patterns with only a few major pieces. Little pieces can be squeezed into unbelievable spaces.

2. Will you use **all** the pattern pieces? Barbara eliminates in-seam pockets from soft skirts because she doesn't want the extra bulk at the hipline. The absence of those four pieces (two per pocket) can

alter the pattern layout to your advantage. If you want pockets, plan to cut them from lining, like Pati and Marta do.

3. Eliminating the hem allowance on a skirt can save more than $5! It's really OK to hem either of these fabrics with **just a cut edge.** In fact, we all prefer this method. Or you can edgestitch (and topstitch) the raw edge, if you prefer a more "finished" look. If you really want a turned hem, allow for only a 3/8" turn up, then topstitch. You'll still be saving fabric since most hems on fuller styles allow for a 2"-wide hem.

4. Do a trial layout (page 10), **before** you buy the fabric to determine exactly how much yardage you'll need. Like Ultrasuede, you can tilt pattern pieces as much as 45° without a noticeable color difference. Leave the pieces pinned in place until you're ready to transfer them to your Facile or Caress or do a sketch or take an instant photo so you don't forget your new layout.

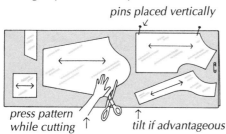

pins placed vertically

press pattern while cutting   *tilt if advantageous*

5. Pieces normally cut on the bias can be cut on the crosswise instead, since the stretch is similar.

6. Consider piecing large pattern sections to better fit the yardage. After all, genuine suede is usually pieced because the skins are small. Take advantage of suede's popularity in current fashion and "snoop-shop" in designer departments and boutiques for piecing ideas for a genuine suede look. Our favorite full, flared, pull-on, skirt takes lots less yardage when cut as shown here—just a little more than two yards instead of the 3 1/4+ yards the pattern calls for when it's cut on the cross grain!!! That amounts to substantial savings!

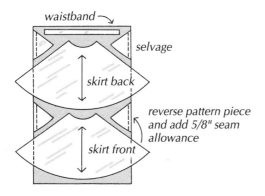

waistband

selvage

skirt back

reverse pattern piece and add 5/8" seam allowance

skirt front

Suitable Shaping Fabrics

Fusible interfacings, especially weft-insertion types are ideal. Our favorites for Facile and Caress are Armo Whisper Weft and Armo Weft, a bit heavier. Soft 'N Silky is a new lightweight warp insertion that's similar to Whisper Weft. Don't just take our word for it. **Test** a few options on scraps before fusing interfacing to garment pieces. See the information on choosing and applying fusible interfacing on pages 26-28.

Because Facile and Caress are usually sewn into soft, unstructured designs, a **lining is optional.** However, Marta completely lines soft jackets. And she makes "linings" for culottes as separate "culotte slips." For comfort's sake in warmer climates you might want to line only the sleeves of soft jackets. See page 101. A more structured or fitted jacket or coat made from Facile should be fully lined for added body and better wear.

Fabric Preparation

In testing both these fabrics, there was no measurable shrinkage, so preshrinking is not necessary. If your sewing machine is prone to skipped stitches, however, prewashing sometimes helps stop the problem.

Because you will probably launder your finished Facile or Caress garment, it is essential that all components—zippers, tapes, applied trims—are also washable. They should be preshrunk if not marked as such. Preshrink fusible interfacings and washable linings as directed for Ultrasuede garments on page 21.

Pattern Fitting

As with Ultrasuede, prefitting the pattern is essential and the same information and fitting techniques apply to Facile and Caress.

> **QUICK TIP:** You can baste seams and darts for a fitting in these fabrics without worry of the holes remaining. Fine pin and needle holes will "heal" when steam is applied. **Do not press seams open until the fit is finalized**. It's very difficult, if not impossible, to get crease lines out.

Cutting and Marking Remarks

Facile and Caress can be cut double layer for speed. Fold the fabric with RIGHT SIDES TOGETHER so the seams are in the "ready-to-sew" position.

Long, glass-headed pins are easier to push into these dense fabrics and fine ones leave smaller holes. You might enjoy using a rotary mat and cutter with pattern weights. Otherwise use a very sharp, long, bent-handled shears.

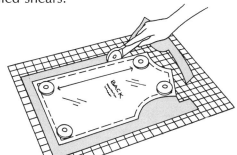

Cut off the notches, then snip mark for faster cutting and better matching accuracy. You can also use any of the marking methods described on pages 21-22 to indicate darts, hemlines and other matching symbols on Facile or Caress.

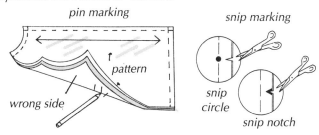

You might want to mark the WRONG SIDE of Facile and Caress scraps with transparent tape to avoid mixups later on. In some colors of these lighter weight fabrics, it' very difficult to tell right from wrong. In fact, you might want to mark the wrong side of every cut piece of your garment **before** removing pattern tissue, just to be safe!

Sewing Tips

In most ways, sewing Facile and Caress is no different than sewing any other fabric. Needle and presser foot choice are the most crucial to stitching success.

Use Schmetz universal point needles, a "cross" between sharp and ballpoint needles. Size 12/80 works best. Like Ultrasuede, Facile and Caress may stick to the standard presser foot so use "**taut sewing,**" or one of the special presser feet shown on page 32 to help seams feed evenly and smoothly.

> **NOTE:** For Singer machines and some others of Japanese manufacture, use Singer "Yellow Band" needles to prevent skipped stitches. If in doubt, consult your machine manual or dealer.

Sewing the Pieces Together

In general, we recommend **conventional** sewing methods for these two fabrics. Because they are lighter weight than Ultrasuede, it's easier to press seams and to turn enclosed seams in collars and cuffs but it's just as important to use the appropriate pressing tools and techniques (pages 24-25).

Flat construction with lapped seams is an option with Facile, but we don't recommend it for Caress. All that topstitching tends to "overwork" it and detract from its beautiful, fluid nature. Also consider the style. A pattern with lots of draping and softness doesn't lend itself to sportier lapped seams.

Follow the construction sequence on your pattern guide with the following tips in mind.

1. If you get **skipped stitches** or puckering, try a new needle and use "taut sewing." Replace the zigzag plate with a straight-stitch needle plate or cover the needle slot of your zigzag plate with masking tape.

2. For **enclosed seams**, be sure to grade seam allowances to reduce bulk. You can trim to 1/16" without worry about raveling. Trim as neatly as possible for a neater appearance and more even topstitching.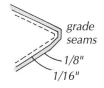

3. **To prevent stretch,** stabilize V-necklines, jacket roll lines, tops of pockets and other crosswise or bias areas with twill tape or the new lightweight "Stay Tape" by Seams Great.

3. **Cord buttonholes** for added dimension, extra strength and to prevent stretch. See page 82. If the ends of buttonholes draw up under the stitching when bartacking, use a small piece of "tear-away" stabilizer under the buttonhole during stitching. Then carefully tear it away from behind; fiber remnants will wash out in the first laundering.

4. **Consider flat construction** when making patch pockets in Facile and steam-baste them in place before edgestitching. See page 85.

5. **SAVE THOSE SCRAPS**—for accessories, gift items, piping or band trims, applique or color blocking on creative garments of your own design.

Waistband—Conventional Method

Use the conventional method for waistbands on both Facile and Caress for better wear. The flat method on page 47 is best for Ultrasuede. We recommend Armoflexxx or Ban-Rol waistband interfacing for conventional waistband treatments on both fabrics. These lightweight monofilament interfacings are available by the yard in up to 2" widths. They will not stretch, roll or wrinkle. Here's how to apply them.

Cut

1. Discard the waistband pattern piece and cut the waistband from the fabric, making it 6" longer than your waistline measurement and twice as wide as the Armoflexxx **plus** 1 1/4" (two 5/8"-wide seam allowances).

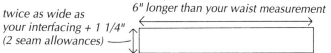

twice as wide as your interfacing + 1 1/4" (2 seam allowances)

6" longer than your waist measurement

Sew

1. Machine baste 5/8" from the long edge on the waistband half that will be visible on the finished garment. **Make sure the nap matches the nap direction of the garment.**

seam line

waistband

2. Stitch the interfacing to the seam allowance on the WRONG SIDE of the band with one edge along the machine basting. (This step produces a completely smooth, ridge-free appearance on the right side).

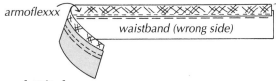

armoflexxx

waistband (wrong side)

Fit and Stitch

1. Wrap the waistband around interfacing. Fit band around your waist. Snip edge of seam allowances where band meets **comfortably**. This is the center back (CB) if you have a back opening or center front (CF) for a fly front opening.

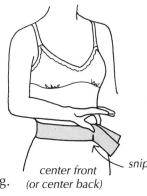

center front (or center back) *snip*

2. Mark the band halfway between the snips for center front (or center back).

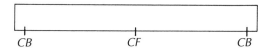

CB   *CF*   *CB*

3. Pin the band to the garment, matching the top edges of band and garment. The interfacing will extend beyond the top edges. Place pins horizontally **on the seamline** at the edge of interfacing so you can try the garment on to check the fit.

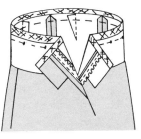

> **FIT TIP:** In fitted garments, the waistline edge of the garment should be slightly larger than the band. Easing the garment onto the band creates a more graceful fit over the curve of tummy and hips.

4. Fold the waistband to the inside and try on the garment. Adjust to fit as needed. Remove garment.

5. Stitch band to garment, stitching from the band side along the edge of the interfacing and removing pins as you stitch. Remove pins as you sew. Do not stitch through the interfacing! The feed dogs will help ease the garment onto the waistband.

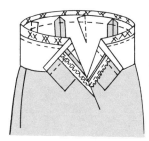

stitch below interfacing edge

Finish

1. Decide how much underlap and overlap you want and trim away the excess. Be sure to leave seam allowances. The amount of overlap and underlap is up to you. You can sew the overlap

side 1/16" from the center front or back and the underlap 1" from the zipper, or leave a 1" extension on both ends.

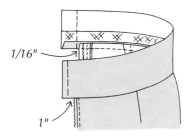

2. Fold band in half, RIGHT SIDES TOGETHER. Trim interfacing to stitching line. Stitch next to the interfacing. Trim seams to 1/4". Turn right side out.

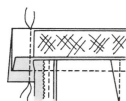

QUICK TIP: Before turning, wrap a 2"-wide piece of fusible web around the interfacing at both ends of the waistband. Turn band right side out and fuse so both sides of interfacing are caught to the waistband. This keeps hooks and eyes from pulling and showing on outside of finished band.

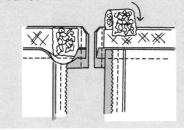

3. On the INSIDE, make a 5/8"-deep clip at the raw edge of the waistband just past the zipper tape. Turn under the seam allowance from the ends of the band to the clips. Slipstitch in place. Pin remainder of the waistband in place.

"Stitch in the ditch" from the RIGHT SIDE hiding the stitches in the well of the waistline seam.

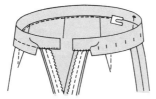

5. Sew on hook and eye and a snap or use a button or snap closure.

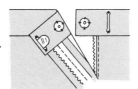

Quick and Easy Pull-on Facile or Caress Skirt

If your hip measurement is 40" or less, you can make a simple skirt from less than a yard of Facile or Caress in less than 30 minutes! You will need a piece of 45"-wide fabric that measures the desired finished length **plus** 3 1/2".

1. Fold and stitch a tube, leaving an 8" opening at one end for walking slit. Press seam open. Fuse opening edges in place with fusible web. Reinforce top of slit as shown.

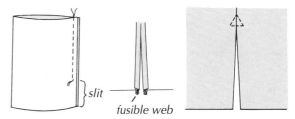

slit   fusible web

2. Pin 1"-wide elastic around waist comfortably. Try skirt on with seam at center back, adjusting fullness evenly around waist under elastic. Adjust to desired length **so skirt hangs parallel to floor all around.** Mark waistline location on skirt at bottom of elastic. Remove skirt.

3. Trim upper edge to an even 2 3/4" from waistline marking all around. Press 1 1/2" to inside. You may have to ease skirt into the casing a bit. Edgestitch. Stitch 1 1/4" from pressed edge to form casing, leaving opening for inserting elastic. Trim excess casing 1/4" below stitching.

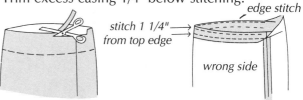

edge stitch

stitch 1 1/4" from top edge

wrong side

4. Cut elastic waistline measurement **plus** 2". Thread elastic through casing. Pin. Adjust fit. Remove skirt. Overlap and stitch elastic ends together in an "X" as shown.

CHAPTER 26:
Sewing With Ultraleather

Ultraleather is the newest addition to the Ultrasuede family of fabulous fabrics. It's a nonwoven fabric with a face of 100% polyurethane on a softly napped knit backing of 70% cuprammonium rayon and 30% nylon that's quite comfortable next to the skin. Available in a nice range of basic neutral colors and exciting new brights, the surface has a slight grain, like the "real thing." Ultraleather's soft and supple hand and luxurious appearance belie its easy-care. Water-repellent and wrinkle-free, it's a wonderful fabric for travel wardrobes and can be washed or dry-cleaned by conventional methods.

Ultraleather is comfortable to wear. It has some give in all directions but it has 100% recovery so it doesn't bag or stretch out of shape.

Best of all, Ultraleather is easier to sew than genuine leather. Conventional seams work beautifully. In fact, flat construction is not recommended as the knit backing will show at the raw edges. **Fine pins** won't leave pinholes and careful steaming from the wrong side will usually reseal needle holes left after removing stitching.

Pattern Selection and Preparation

Check out ready-to-wear leather fashions for design inspiration when choosing a pattern. We've seen terrific pencil-slim skirts and smashing stirrup pants sewn in Ultraleather that would rival any real leather garments in fashion appeal. Because of its excellent stretch and recovery, fitted garments in Ultraleather don't bag out permanently in the seat and knees like real leather. Shaped and fitted jackets as well as tailored and casual styles are another option. **You can also use knit patterns that require no more than 25% stretch,** as well as patterns designed for wovens and leathers.

Ultraleather can be **gently** gathered or tucked but this will add a little bulk to your figure. Opt for designs with seams and darts for shaping and fit rather than lots of tucks or gathers.

Plan to piece Ultraleather on purpose (see Marta's skirt on page 74) to make it look even more like the real thing. Save your scraps for belts and bags. Ultraleather combines beautifully with wovens and

knits as trim—beautiful bindings, creative appliques and classy patchwork. Marta's black cashmere jacket (page 74) is simply smashing with its Ultraleather binding and welt pocket!

Fit and adjust the pattern before cutting. See page 29.

Shaping Fabrics

Interfacings—Choose interfacings by doing a test sample. As with Ultrasuede, you can use fusible interfacings on the wrong side of Ultraleather. Fusible knits are the ideal choice for adding body while retaining the inherent stretch in the fabric. **Fuse only from the wrong side when applying fusible interfacings to Ultraleather.**

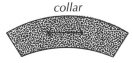
collar

Cut collar interfacings with the stretch going around the neckline for a soft roll.

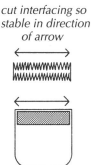
cut interfacing so stable in direction of arrow

Use the stable, lengthwise grain of the interfacing in the same direction buttonholes will be stitched and across the top edges of pockets to control stretch. For areas where you want more stability and body, try a weft-insertion interfacing or a stable nonwoven.

Linings—Linings are optional in Ultraleather. A lining will lessen stretching while wearing more fitted garments, but since Ultraleather has 100% stretch recovery, that may not be a consideration. Line a very fitted straight skirt to relieve stress on the seams. Since the knit backing on Ultraleather tends to stick to other fabrics, you may prefer to line jackets and coats to make them easier to slip on and off. Be sure to choose a washable lining fabric. Lining only the sleeves in a jacket is another option. See page 101.

PRO TIP: Try a static-free nylon tricot lining for an Ultraleather skirt if you don't like the rustling noise of other lining fabrics.

Fabric Preparation

Preshrink Ultraleather to remove any finishing resins on the surface which can cause skipped stitches. Shrinkage, which occurs in the dryer, not the washer, is about 1/2" to 1" per yard in length **and** width in Ultraleather. Preshrink as you will care for the finished garment. Machine wash with a mild detergent and tumble dry at a low heat. Remove finished Ultraleather garments from the dryer while slightly damp to avoid overdrying the thread which can cause permanently puckered seams. Hang on a padded hanger to finish drying. Preshrink all findings as well.

Cutting and Marking Tips

Ultraleather cuts like butter with either sharp shears or a rotary cutter and mat. Since it has no nap and it's also 48" wide, you can rearrange cutting layouts to save on yardage, tilting pattern pieces, even cutting some on the opposite "grainline" when the direction of stretch doesn't matter.

To save yardage, cut bias grainlines on the crossgrain where Ultraleather has the most give. When using a knit pattern be sure to plan the layout so Ultraleather's crosswise stretch goes **around** the body. We recommend doing a trial pattern layout **before** purchasing the fabric. Savings can be substantial, even when you save just 1/4 yard in the layout.

1. Fold Ultraleather with WRONG SIDES together. The knit backing grabs onto itself and the layers are less likely to slip and slide out of place while cutting.

2. Hold pattern pieces in place with pattern weights, **removable** transparent tape or a spray-on adhesive such as Pattern-Sta. Or use **very fine** pins only within the seam allowances; large pinholes may not steam out.

3. Because you use conventional construction, snip-mark notches and other symbols along pattern edges. Transfer other symbols using any of the methods shown for Ultrasuede on page 22.

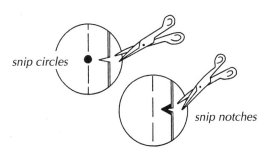

snip circles

snip notches

Sewing and Pressing Tips for Ultraleather

1. Use size 12 (80) universal sewing machine needles. **Do not use leather needles.** Their larger holes weaken seams and are impossible to remove if you make a stitching error.

2. Use **conventional** seams and hems since the knit backing on Ultraleather would show at the cut edges in flat construction.

3. Stitch seams, right sides together, with the machine set for 10 stitches per inch. Lengthen the stitch to 6 to 8 stitches per inch for topstitching. Use taut sewing (page 32) to prevent slippage while stitching.

4. Press seams open using a heavy muslin, **napped or woolen press cloth,** lots of steam and the tailor's clapper to flatten them. To keep seams open permanently, fuse 1/4"-wide strips of fusible web between the garment and seam allowance with one edge of the web at the seamline.

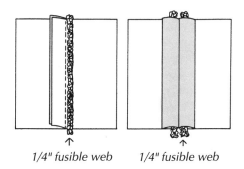

1/4" fusible web   *1/4" fusible web*

QUICK TIP: Fusing the seam allowances in place gives you the option of sewing an Ultraleather garment with conventional seams without the necessity of topstitching them to keep them permanently flat. It also makes it possible to topstitch them from the right side without the presser foot sticking, dragging and stretching the top layer causing puckered, wrinkled seams.

Fusing the seams down doesn't seem to add any noticeable stiffness to the seams. If you don't fuse them, you will need to use taut sewing or one of the special presser feet discussed on page 32 to prevent needle drag and seam slippage problems.

5. Topstitch seams after fusing in place (Tip 4) if desired. Stitch 1/4" away on each side of seamline. Use edge of presser foot as a guide.

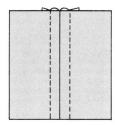

If you prefer, press and fuse seam allowances to one side. Trim seam allowance closest to garment to a scant 1/4" to eliminate bulk. Topstitch from the right side.

For the look of flat-felled seams, press allowances to one side. Stitch close to seamline through all layers, then topstitch 1/4" away.

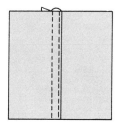

6. Slash darts and press open over a ham. Fuse edges in place as shown for seams.

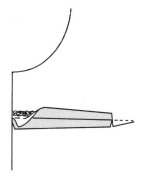

7. Always use a press cloth when pressing Ultraleather and press on the WRONG SIDE **only.** Be careful not to stretch the Ultraleather while pressing.

PRO TIP: In bulky areas where seams intersect each other, it may be necessary to take slightly deeper seams to prevent them from pooching out. Marta found this necessary in her pieced skirt.

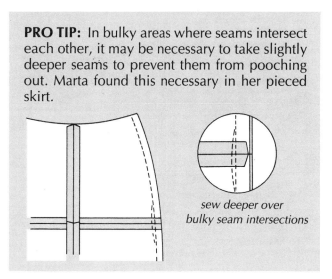

sew deeper over bulky seam intersections

Zipper

Invisible zippers are the perfect choice for Ultraleather because they're fast, require no basting or topstitching and simply disappear into the seam.

Our second choice is a **centered zipper** which requires a little special handling. Use a lightweight, synthetic coil zipper.

QUICK TIP: For the easiest zipper application, use a zipper 2" longer than the actual opening. After applying the zipper, **unzip the zipper,** apply the waistband or facing and cut away the excess zipper above the waistline edge. Today's synthetic zippers self-lock when the pull tab is pushed down so you can shorten them from the top.

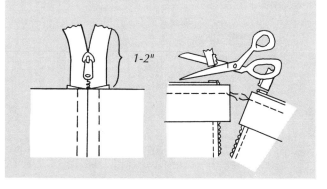

1-2"

1. Stitch the seam ending at the zipper opening. **Do not backstitch.** Pull the threads to the wrong side, tie a dressmaker's overhand knot and secure with a dab of Fray Check. **Do not baste** the zipper opening closed to avoid needle holes in the folded edges of the zipper opening.

2. Turn under and press the 5/8" seam allowance in zipper opening. Fuse seam allowances in place for smooth topstitching with narrow strips of fusible web. If you plan to topstitch seam below the zipper, continue fusing seam allowances to garment below opening.

fusible web

3. On RIGHT SIDE, butt pressed edges of opening together and tape securely with 1/2"-wide **removable transparent tape** centered over the two edges.

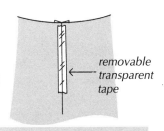

removable transparent tape

PRO TIP: The only tape we recommend for use on the right side of Ultraleather is **removable transparent tape,** available at most office supply stores. Other tapes can pull away the surface.

4. Cut 1/4"-wide strips of Pellon® Wonder Under™ transfer web and apply to the RIGHT SIDE of outer edges of zipper tape following manufacturer's directions. Peel away protective paper.

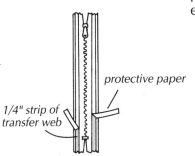

protective paper

1/4" strip of transfer web

NOTE: Trans-web™ by HTC is 3/4" wide. It can be cut in half and substituted for the strips of Wonder Under.

5. On INSIDE of garment, center the zipper, face down, over the seamline and fuse to the seam allowances, using a dampened press cloth. The zipper slide should be **above** the cut edge of garment, out of the way of topstitching.

6. On the RIGHT SIDE, topstitch zipper in place, stitching along edges of tape. Stitch both halves in the same direction, continuing topstitching along remainder of seam if desired. Remove tape.

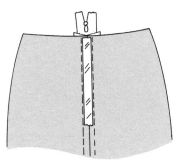

Hems

Hems are easy in Ultraleather. Simply turn, press and fuse, adding topstitching detail if desired. You can also handstitch hems in place catching the stitches to the knit backing only—much more time-consuming!!!

1. For **straight hems,** turn and press a 1/2"- to 1"-wide hem. Cut a strip of fusible web the hem width, less 1/4". Position web with one edge at the hemline fold and fuse the hem allowance to the garment using a damp press cloth. Do not press over the top edge of the hem to avoid an edge imprint on the right side.

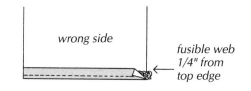

wrong side

fusible web 1/4" from top edge

2. Trim **shaped hems** to a width of no more than 1". Partially ease out the fullness with easestitching 1/4" from the raw edge. Cut fusible web and fuse as described for straight hems. Do not press past the easestitching.

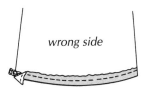

wrong side

Details, Details

Conventional sewing methods work best for the details in Ultraleather garments.

Waistbands—Use the conventional method as shown for Facile and Caress (page 110).

Pockets—Try conventional patch pockets following the pattern guidesheet or for more design interest, single or double welt pockets (page 86) are wonderful in Ultraleather.

patch pockets   single welt pocket   double welt pocket

Buttons and buttonholes—Make either conventional machine stitched buttonholes or the conventional windowpane bound buttonhole (as illustrated in *Easy, Easier, Easiest Tailoring* by Pati Palmer and Susan Pletch.) For machine stitched buttonholes, make a test first. If the layers shift while stitching, fuse the facing to the garment in the buttonhole area before making the buttonhole, fusing from the WRONG SIDE and using a press cloth.

conventional machine stitched   conventional window pane bound buttonhole

Add a reinforcement button under those buttons that will get a lot of use—in a coat or jacket topper, for example, stitch in place at the same time you sew on your fashion button.

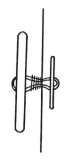

Jacket or coat lining—Use the conventional quick lining method, page 100.

Binding—Cut Ultraleather binding from scrap in any direction.

1. Decide on the desired finished width. Cut and piece enough strips for the project. Make strips 3 times the desired finished width **plus 3/8".** Piece strips on the diagonal as you would true bias for a professional, nonbulky finish.

line up here

> **PRO TIP:** Finished widths of no more than 1" are easiest to handle on curved edges.

2. Pin to the garment edge, RIGHT SIDES together, and stitch the desired finished width from the raw edge.

3. Wrap the binding around the raw edge, steam press lightly and edgestitch or stitch in the well of the seam to catch the raw edge of the binding.

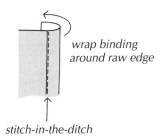

wrap binding around raw edge

stitch-in-the-ditch

CHAPTER 27:
Creative Ideas for the Ultrasuede Family of Fabrics

What do you do with the larger pieces of the Ultrasuede fabrics you've so cleverly managed to save with careful layout and cutting? We love them all— Ultrasuede, Ultraleather, Facile and Caress—used as accents on other garments to create beautiful designer details. One of Marta's favorite projects was a wonderful, soft Facile skirt and a wool cardigan jacket trimmed with matching Facile binding around the neckline edge. Ultraleather makes great binding, too. See page 117 for basic binding tips appropriate for all of these fabrics.

Perhaps you've saved a piece of Ultrasuede large enough for the front of a waist-length jacket. Combine it with other washable knit or woven fabrics for a "multi-media" design. Try a "sweatshirt" jacket with Facile or Ultraleather for the jacket body and wool jersey for the sleeves and back neck and front bands.

Cut elbow patches, pockets, belts, yokes, collars and cuffs from scrap yardage for accents on woven or knit garments. Don't overdo it, though. A good rule of thumb—use an accent in three places so the look doesn't get too spotty—collar, cuffs and a pocket, for example. Covered buttons are another possibility.

Pipe It!

Ultrasuede or Ultraleather piping adds a special designer touch—on the shawl collar of a jacket, at the edge of a yoke or on pockets and belts, for example. It's a nice accent on knife-edge toss pillows for home dec projects, too.

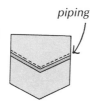

piping

Use **flat piping** for bound button-hole lips or for trimming yokes, pockets, collars and belts. Cut 1"- to 1 1/2"-wide strips of any of the Ultrasuede fabrics. **Cut on the crosswise grain for the most give to go around shaped or curved areas.** Fold in half, WRONG SIDES TOGETHER, and steam-baste raw edges together. **Corded piping** adds more dimension. Wrap piping strip around a string or preshrunk cording. Use your regular zipper foot or

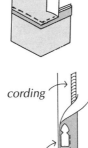

cording

zipperfoot

assemble your invisible zipper foot and position a "tunnel" on bottom so needle will stitch just next to cord. Machine stitch.

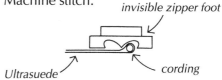

invisible zipper foot

Ultrasuede *cording*

> **PRO TIP:** To piece strips of Ultrasuede or Facile, cut the ends at a 45° angle, overlap, steam-baste and edgestitch. **Piece Caress and Ultraleather with conventional seams.**
>
>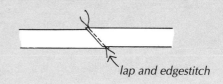
>
> *lap and edgestitch*

Patchwork Pizazz

Create your own fabric from scraps to use as trim or to make a whole new piece of fabric for a tote bag, a yoke, cuff or pocket—even an entire garment like the jacket pictured on page 76.

Overlap, steam-baste and stitch as in flat construction, or stitch with decorative machine stitches like hand stitched crazy quilting.

> **DESIGNER TIP:** Use patchwork designs from reference books or just play with existing scrap pieces, cutting and overlapping related shapes in a random fashion to create a pleasing design. Use pattern pieces as a guide to create separate pieces of fabric just large enough for each garment piece.
>
>

Quilt It, Too!

For added dimension and elegance, quilt a piece of plain or patchwork Ultrasuede, Facile, or Ultraleather **before** cutting a garment or accessory from it. Marta quilted the fabric for her red Ultraleather jacket (page 74) in no time! She loves to quilt her Ultrasuede handbags, too. See page 78 and 79 for ideas.

For garment pieces, plan and design the patchwork on top of batting or fleece. Tuck narrow strips of fusible web under edges of fabric only where you plan to stitch. Steam-baste. Stitch permanently.

For added body in smaller accessories, layer and fuse fabric, fusible web and fleece. Quilt in geometric patterns. Diamonds, squares and channels are easiest to mark and stitch. Try quilting with a double needle and straight or serpentine stitching.

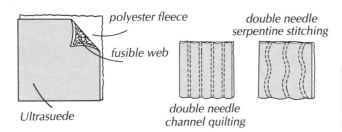

polyester fleece

fusible web

double needle serpentine stitching

Ultrasuede

double needle channel quilting

Trapunto Adds Dimension

Trapunto is an Italian variation of quilting used to add design interest and dimension to the surface of smooth fabrics. Barbara's simple Ultraleather jacket (page 73) was a perfect background for this decorative technique.

1. Plan design with areas that can be padded and corded. Transfer to a lightweight, firmly woven backing fabric cut slightly larger all around than design. Glue-baste to garment in desired position on WRONG SIDE, applying glue sparingly only to outer edges.

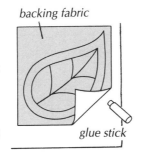

backing fabric

glue stick

2. Stitch on design lines through all layers. Thread cord or yarn through channels on a tapestry needle. Insert needle into backing between rows of stitching. For curves and angles, bring needle out and reinsert at same place leaving a little cording out to prevent buckling or puckering. Trim cord ends to 1/8".

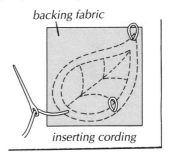

backing fabric

inserting cording

3. Stuff other design areas. On INSIDE, make a small slit in backing fabric. Stuff small bits of polyester fiberfill into shaped design areas using a knitting needle or a chopstitck to push it into place. Catchstitch slits closed.

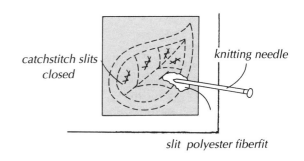

catchstitch slits closed

knitting needle

slit polyester fiberfit

> **QUICK TIP:** Fuse a small piece of interfacing over slits to prevent ravelling. Line the garment to hide the backing—it's not "pretty."

Ultrasuede "Lace"

You can create incredibly beautiful Ultrasuede "lace" with a few simple tools. The collar on Barbara's cardigan jacket (page 65) was done with a revolving leather punch, a scalloping scissors and an eyelet punch. Sketch your own designs or adapt design ideas from paper doilies, design books for machine cutwork, actual lace, or lace designs in reference books on antique lace.

Embellish your lace with machine embroidery stitches where appropriate. Start with something small—perhaps the flap on a clutch bag. Add "lace" cuffs to a blouse or the edge of a pair of gloves. Make placemats with cutouts. Have fun experimenting with cutwork ideas on small scraps!

1. Develop design and draw it freehand on WRONG SIDE of garment section. Or trace it onto stiff paper or lightweight cardboard, then cut and/or punch it out to create a stencil you can trace onto the WRONG SIDE with a fine waterproof pen. Position design inside seam allowances in areas that get the least wearing strain.

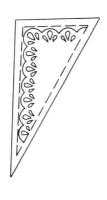

2. Use the leather punch and eyelet punch for holes of varying sizes and to "start" larger designs that can be scissors-cut. For sharp, clean holes, place an Ultrasuede or real leather scrap under the fabric so you're punching through two layers. This helps punch stay sharp longer.

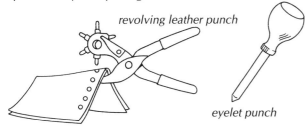

revolving leather punch

eyelet punch

3. Cut tiny petal shapes and slits with **very sharp, double-pointed embroidery scissors.** Use an X-Acto knife or Olfa Touch Knife for larger cutout areas and work on a rotary cutting mat.

4. Cut interesting shapes along outer edges. Try pinking or scalloping edges, too.

5. If you make an overcut, either change the design to incorporate it or use a toothpick to apply a little Sobo glue to the area on the wrong side and allow to dry. Sobo dries clear and won't wash out.

Applique is Easy

Create a work of art with the little bits and pieces you couldn't bear to throw away. Look for design ideas in mail-order catalogs and needlework and craft magazines. Applique adds design interest to the collar and yoke of Terri Burns' machine knit jacket on page 69.

Applique shapes can be simply edgestitched in place, shaped and tacked in place for three-dimensional accents, or embellished with machine embroidery or decorative serging. The appliqued leaf shape on Barbara's strapless Caress bustier in the photo inset on page 73 was embellished with decorative machine embroidery **before** sewing it in place. Serger piping and rolled edge chain add more design interest. For lots of wonderful serger ideas, see **"The Serger Idea Book"** by Palmer/Pletsch Associates. See page 127.

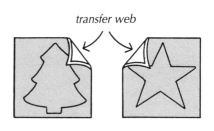

3-dimensional applique

1. Sketch and finalize design and mark location on garment. Cut paper patterns for each shape. Or cut freehand shapes like Marta does.

2. Apply fusible transfer web such as Wonder Under to WRONG SIDE of fabric for each shape following manufacturer's directions. Fabric should be slightly larger than finished size of applique shape. Cut shapes from the backed fabrics.

transfer web

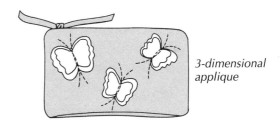

3. Remove backing paper and fuse applique in position on garment, following manufacturer's directions. **Use a wool or napped press cloth.** Edgestitch.

PRO TIP: The extra body that the web adds is often desirable when doing applique with Facile or Caress. However when overlapping Ultrasuede shapes, you may not want the added body of the transfer web throughout the design. If so, tuck strips of fusible web under the edges only and fuse. Test first!

DESIGNER TIP: Create lacy cutwork designs in Ultrasuede or Facile to "applique" to Ultrasuede garments or garments made from other fabrics. Back the suede with transfer web before cutting the lace, then position, fuse and edgestitch. For reverse applique, do cutwork in the actual garment or accessory and lay other colors behind. Edgestitch.

lacy cutwork applique

The edges on the pockets and facings of Barbara's Facile "sweater" jacket (page 72) were finished with decorative serging and topstitched in place, much like an applique, rather than sewn to the inside of the jacket as the pattern guidesheet showed. She set the serger for a close, balanced stitch and used a beautiful rayon Decor 6 thread in the upper looper. After serging the edges, she simply positioned the pockets and steam-basted them in place, then edgestitched through the outer edge of the serger stitches.

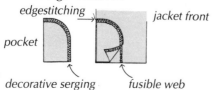

edgestitching   *jacket front*

pocket

decorative serging   *fusible web*

Weaving With Ultrasuede and Facile

Cut fabric into "ribbons" and weave it into a new fabric like Marta did for the yoke of a child's dress (page 77) and the pocket on her colorful drawstring bag (page 79).

1. Cut and apply Pellon Wonder Under or HTC Trans-Web™ (transfer web) to WRONG SIDE of fabric pieces for weaving. **Do not remove backing paper.**

2. Mark desired width of weaving strips onto backed fabrics and cut with sharp shears or use a rotary cutter, ruler and mat to measure and cut them. Widths of 1/4" to 1/2" are best. **Remove backing paper.**

3. Weave strips into desired pattern and shape. Anchor ends to cutting board with pins. To prevent strips from shifting and to add body, fuse completed weaving to a piece of lightweight woven fabric that matches or blends with the weaving. **Use a napped or wool press cloth.** For additional body in handbags, fuse the backed weaving to polyester fleece.

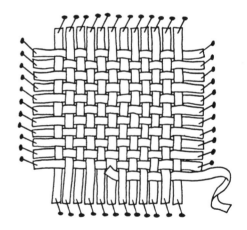

4. Cut weaving into desired shape and complete construction of the garment or accessory.

You Can Knit with Facile or Caress!

When Marta found out it was possible to make your own "yarn" from Facile or Caress, she taught herself to knit. Now that's dedication! Her simple sweater shapes combine regular hand knitting yarns with hand-cut strips of Facile in stripes and random patterns. See some of her handiwork pictured on page 67.

To make your own suede "yarn," cut 1/8"- to 1/4"-wide continuous strips from selvage to selvage. Beginning at one selvage, cut first strip, stopping about 1/4" from edge of opposite selvage. Move over the desired width and cut back **to but not through** the opposite selvage. Continue cutting in this zigzag fashion, winding the "yarn" into balls as you go.

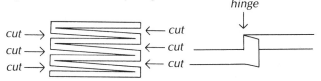

NOTE: The "hinges" left at each selvage edge of your "yarn" won't break, will work right into the knitting and aren't obvious in the finished piece. Don't worry about making the strips a uniform width. "It's not important," says Marta.

Use size 8 or 9 knitting needles and choose other yarns to coordinate with your "yarn" that knit to the same qauge. It may take a little experimentation.

Terri Burns, creative machine knitter extraordinaire, used strips of Caress in her sweater pictured on page 69. She simply laid them into the design, catching the strips into every fifth stitch as she knit back and forth across the machine. Very clever and very effective! Strips were cut 3/8" wide on the lengthwise grain. Strips cut crosswise caused skipped stitch problems in machine knitting. Crosswise cutting does work for hand knitting, however.

Fringe It!

Ultrasuede and Facile are perfect for fringed details on shirts, shawls, handbags and belts. Marta's white shawl (page 78 and 79) is simply two lengths of Facile seamed together, then slashed at both ends. The fringed handbag (page 78) is an easy 30-minute project! Just do an exposed zipper (page 47) on the diagonal of a square of fabric. Fold in half, WRONG SIDES TOGETHER, steam-baste and fuse. Slash both layers to stitching to create "fringe." Add simple shoulder straps.

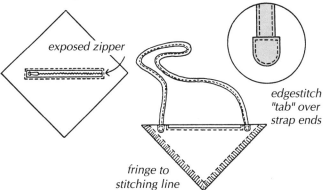

exposed zipper

edgestitch "tab" over strap ends

fringe to stitching line

Make Ultrasuede tassels, too. Cut a small rectangle and clip at 1/8" to 1/4" intervals to within 1/4" of one edge. Roll and secure with a few stitches or with Sobo glue.

Designing With Color Blocking and Nap Reversal

We love to personalize Ultrasuede garment designs by making minor changes to patterns. Barbara cut the front pattern piece for her simple Facile tee-shirt (page 72) into two pieces, adding seam allowances at the cut edges and the center front. Then she cut the pieces so the nap was reversed from piece to piece for an interesting play of light. Decorative serging finishes the lapped seam edges.

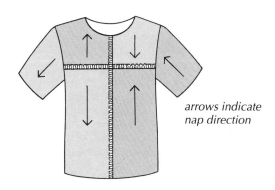

arrows indicate nap direction

Marta's tri-color Facile top shown with Ultraleather stretch pants on page 77 was color-blocked in much the same way by cutting the pattern pieces first from pattern tracing cloth to work out the design. Then the pieces were cut from different colors and fused and sewn with lapped seams (flat construction).

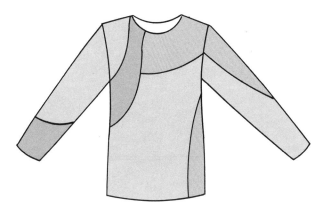

Don't Stop Now!

As the song goes, "you've only just begun." We hope we have made your first or most recent adventure sewing with Ultrasuede fabrics an enjoyable, rewarding and fun experience. We know your time spent has been a wise investment.

We have enjoyed sewing and wearing Ultrasuede for almost twenty years and have recently enjoyed the versatility of the new generation of microfiber fabrics with the addition of Facile, Caress, and Ultraleather to the Ultrasuede family. If you haven't yet tried them all, we encourage you to make your next garment from one of the Ultrasuede "cousins". We know you'll be glad you did! For now, give yourself a pat on the back for your fashion sense and daring. Keep up the good work!

Barbara
Marta   Pati

Barbara, Marta, and Pati

P.S. If you'd like to see Ultrasuede techniques shown in this book come alive on the screen, consider adding our companion video to your library. See page 127 for additional information.

Index

ADDITIONAL PRODUCTS FROM PALMER/PLETSCH

Palmer/Pletsch publishes easy to use, information-filled sewing how-to books. Look for our books and videos in local fabric stores or order through Palmer/Pletsch.

BOOKS

☐ **The Serger Idea Book**—A Collection of Inspiring Ideas from Palmer/Pletsch, 8½" × 11", 160 pgs., $16.95 Color photos and how-to's on inspiring and fashionable ideas from the Extraordinary to the Practical.

☐ **Creative Serging for the Home**—And Other Quick Decorating Ideas, by Lynette Ranney Black and Linda Wisner, 8½" × 11", 128 pgs., $16.95 Color photos and how-to's to help you transform your home into the place you want it to be.

☐ **Sewing With Sergers**—The Complete Handbook for Overlock Sewing, by Pati Palmer & Gail Brown, 128 pgs., $6.95 Learn easy threading tips, stitch types, rolled edging and flatlocking on your serger.

☐ **Creative Serging**—The Complete Handbook for Decorative Overlock Sewing, by Pati Palmer, Gail Brown & Sue Green, 128 pgs., $6.95 In-depth information and creative uses of your serger.

☐ **Creative Serging Illustrated,** by Pati Palmer, Gail Brown & Sue Green, 160 pgs., $14.95 Same content as Creative Serging PLUS color photography.

☐ **Sew to Success!**—How to Make Money in a Home-Based Sewing Business, by Kathleen Spike, 128 pgs., $8.95 Learn how to establish your market, set policies and procedures, price your talents and more!

☐ **Mother Pletsch's Painless Sewing,** Revised Edition, by Pati Palmer & Susan Pletsch, 128 pgs., $6.95 The most uncomplicated sewing book of the century! Filled with sewing tips on how to sew FAST!

☐ **Sensational Silk**—A Handbook for Sewing Silk and Silk-like Fabrics, by Gail Brown, 128 pgs., $6.95 Complete guide for sewing with silkies from selection to perfection in sewing.

☐ **Pants For Any Body,** Revised Edition, by Pati Palmer & Susan Pletsch, 128 pgs., $6.95 Learn to fit pants with clear step-by-step problem and solution illustrations.

☐ **Sewing Ultrasuede® Brand Fabrics**—Ultrasuede®, Facile®, Caress™, Ultraleather™, by Marta Alto, Pati Palmer and Barbara Weiland, 8½" × 11", 128 pages, $16.95. Inspiring color fashion photo section, plus the newest techniques to help you master these luxurious fabrics.

☐ **Easy, Easier, Easiest Tailoring,** Revised Edition, by Pati Palmer and Susan Pletsch, 128 pgs., $6.95 Learn 4 different tailoring methods, easy fit tips, and timesaving machine lining.

☐ **Clothes Sense**—Straight Talk About Wardrobe Planning, by Barbara Weiland & Leslie Wood, 128 pgs., $6.95 Learn to define your personal style and when to sew or buy.

☐ **Sew a Beautiful Wedding,** by Gail Brown & Karen Dillon, 128 pgs., $6.95 Bridal how-to's on choosing the most flattering style to sewing with specialty fabrics.

☐ **Decorating with Fabric:** An Idea Book, by Judy Lindahl, 128 pgs., $6.95 Learn to cover walls, create canopies, valances, pillows, lamp shades, and more!

☐ **The Shade Book,** by Judy Lindahl, 128 pgs., $6.95 Learn six major shade types and variations of them, trimmings, hardware, hemming, care, and upkeep.

☐ **Energy Saving Decorating,** by Judy Lindahl, 128 pgs., $6.95 Thoroughly researched techniques for energy efficient windows and walls.

☐ **Original Roo** (The Purple Kangaroo), by Bob Benz, 48 pgs., $4.95 A whimsical children's story about a kangaroo's adventures and how she saves the day with sewing.

VIDEOS

According to Robbie Fanning, author and critic, "The most professional of all the (video) tapes we've seen is Pati Palmer's Sewing Today the Time Saving Way. This tape should serve as the standard of excellence in the field." Following that standard, we have produced 6 more videos since Time Saving! *Videos are $29.95 each.*

☐ **Sewing Today the Time Saving Way,** 45 minutes featuring Lynn Raasch & Karen Dillon sharing tips and techniques to make sewing fun, fast and trouble free.

☐ **Sewing to Success,** 45 minutes featuring Kathleen Spike who presents a wealth of information on how to achieve financial freedom working in your home as a professional dressmaker.

☐ **Sewing With Sergers — Basics,** 1 hour featuring Marta Alto & Pati Palmer on tensions, stitch types and their uses, serging circles, turning corners, gathering and much more.

☐ **Sewing With Sergers—Advanced,** 1 hour featuring Marta Alto & Pati Palmer on in depth how-to's for rolled edging & flatlocking as well as garment details.

☐ **Creative Serging,** 1 hour featuring Marta Alto & Pati Palmer on how to use decorative threads, yarns and ribbons on your serger. PLUS: fashion shots!

☐ **Creative Serging II,** 1 hour featuring Marta Alto & Pati Palmer showing more creative ideas, including in-depth creative rolled edge.

☐ **Sewing Ultrasuede Brand Fabrics—Ultrasuede, Facile, Caress, Ultraleather,** 1 hour featuring Marta Alto and Pati Palmer with clear, step-by-step sewing demonstrations and fashion show.

TREND BULLETINS

Trends Bulletins are comprehensive 8-12 page two-color publications designed to keep you up-to-date by bringing you the best and the newest information on all your favorite sewing topics.

☐ **The Newest in Sewing Room Design,** *by Lynette Ranney Black.* This is the handbook for designing a sewing room covering, proper sewing and pressing heights, layout styles, lighting and more! *$3.50*

☐ **The Newest in Ultrasuede Brand Fabrics,** *by Marta Alto & Ann Price,* gives pattern selection guidance, layout, cutting, and sewing of the new Facile, Caress and Ultraleather. *$3.50*

☐ **Trends in Decorative Threads for the Serger,** *by Ann Price,* gives the most up-to-the minute information on decorative threads including how and where to use them. *$3.50*

☐ **Knitting Machines—An Introduction,** *by Terri Burns,* presents the basics of machine knitting, including stitch patterns, explanation of single and double bed machines, and a step-by-step guide to making your purchasing decision. *$3.95*

☐ **Interfacings,** *by Ann Price,* sorts out all the recent changes, presenting a clear picture of the interfacings available today and how best to make use of them. *$3.95*

Palmer/Pletsch also offers seminars and workshops around the U.S.A. and Canada. Extensive 4-day workshops for the avid sewer are held in Portland, Oregon.

We also carry hard to find and unique notions including Decor 6 Rayon thread and Henckels scissors. Thread color cards are available for $2.00. Check your local fabric store or contact Palmer/Pletsch Associates, P.O. Box 12046, Portland, OR 97212-0046. (503) 274-0687.